I See a Voice

I See a Voice

To John —
who, at the moment,
has time on his hands
(or his leg!) with love from

Jay

August 2017.

Jay Norris

ISBN 978-0-9566684-1-7

Prepared and printed by:

York Publishing Services Ltd
64 Hallfield Road
Layerthorpe
York YO31 7ZQ
Tel: 01904 431213

Website: www.yps-publishing.co.uk

For Paul

(And, yet again, very special thanks to Richard,
for proof-reading and editing the text)

Contents

Chapter 1

I grew up in a comfortable world of women. My father had died in 1926, when I was five and my only sister, Margaret, always called 'Peggy', was thirteen. Our mother, Buddy, was the bread-winner, and made all the important decisions. ("He who pays the piper," she would say, "calls the tune!") She was a State Registered Nurse, and I always knew that the letters SRN were the key to true professional status. The silver badge she wore on her lapel, with its blue enamel edging and her name engraved on the back, had a little chain with a tiny safety pin, to make sure that the badge didn't accidentally fall off. It was her most treasured possession and there was even a colour she always called 'state registered blue'.

Buddy had trained at St Bartholomew's Hospital in London, just before the First World War, and in 1922, became one of the first three thousand nurses to gain state registration. She had a repertoire of amusing little poems about the traumas of nursing training in hospital, and her favourite began:

"Before I came to be a nurse, I thought the work would be
As gloriously great and grand, as it appeared to me.
I thought each Sister was a saint, in sober cap and gown,
A being from some higher sphere, to lesser worlds come down"

The verse went on to describe the reality of the day to day drudgery of being a lowly probationer, but kept the joy that was to be found, finally, in the noble work of caring for the sick. All through my schooldays, Buddy was the Matron at various homes and hospitals, and she never doubted that nursing was a vocation, not just a job. She hoped that I might follow in her footsteps, but was wise enough to see that it was a decision I would have to make for myself.

By the early 1930s, she had become the Matron of 'The British Dental Hospital', and we had settled down to live in Tooting, SW17, a white, working class suburb, on the Underground Northern line. When I got home from school, I often used to go with Buddy into the dental surgery after the last patient had gone and the clinic had closed, and I loved to pump the chair up and down. The foot operated tooth drill swung, on a flexible tube, loosely over the chair, and was the cause of the first real tragedy of my young life.

We had a dear little kitten called 'Tigger', and he jumped up and tried to catch the temptingly moving bit. Unfortunately it brushed against him and immediately caught a little of his fur around the whirling tip. He panicked, and it was impossible to release him unless we could quieten him down. Buddy rose to the occasion, suggesting a 'whiff of gas' as the answer. She quickly got hold of the rubber mask attached to a gas cylinder, that was used for tooth extractions, and as I held the kitten still, she pushed the mask over his little face and turned the gas on. It worked very quickly, and we were able to release the twisted fur, but poor Tigger would never play with anything again. He was dead. The whiff had been an overdose and I was desperately upset.

Just over a year later, I was climbing a tree in the Dental Hospital garden and the branch broke. I put my hand out to stop myself falling, but caught the sharp tip of a corrugated iron fence, which went right into the palm, leaving a deep wound. The doctor thought it would heal without being stitched and he was right, but because the bandage had been put on with the fingers closed, the wound started to heal and my hand could not be opened. I heard Buddy discussing with one of the dental surgeons her determination to give me a 'whiff of gas' and open it under an anaesthetic.

I was horrified, for memories of Tigger's fate were all too fresh in my mind, so I immediately went into the patients' lavatory and forced the fingers straight. The scar broke and the wound gaped, but terror kept me going and a minute later I was able to go to Buddy and show her my open hand. She had to agree that a 'whiff of gas' would not be needed after all!

The roads in Tooting were very busy, with several bus routes and a tramline. There were a lot of shops, like Woolworth's, a Lyons Teashop and a luxurious Odeon-style cinema, called 'The Granada', where Harold Ramsay played the Wurlitzer Organ every day, using George Gershwin's 'Rhapsody In Blue' as his signature tune.

I was sent to the Convent of the Holy Family High School for Girls, just off Tooting Broadway, which was run by an enclosed teaching order of nuns from France. The uniform, navy gym slips, white blouses, school tie and black stockings, was mandatory at all times of the year. When you knelt to pray, the front of your gym slip should just touch the ground, which meant that, when you stood up, it came just below your knees. The outdoor uniform was a navy overcoat in winter, with a velour hat, and in summer, a blazer with a panama. Both hats had a school badge and an elastic to go under your chin, to stop them blowing off. We changed into plimsolls when we arrived in the morning, and only put on our outdoor shoes again when we left at the end of the day.

The nuns never left the convent grounds, so there were lay sisters, who shopped, and cooked and cleaned and did the gardening. No men were allowed into the building, except for workers like plumbers and electricians, and of course, the Catholic priests, who came daily to say mass. I once, tactlessly, remarked to Sister Lucy, the music teacher, that it was hard to understand why anyone would choose to spend their whole life in a convent. She smiled and told me that if only we knew how happy the nuns were, every girl would want to be a nun. It seemed a strange answer at the time, but maybe a life free from all the pressures of day to day living and a vocation to spend this life preparing for the next, made perfectly good sense.

The sounds of the convent are still with me. The shuffle of slippers, as the nuns walked along the polished wood corridors, the soft clink of the rosary beads that hung from their waists and the distant hum of voices from the chapel, were the background of every day at school. A loudly clanging bell was used to call any particular member of the community, and each sister had her own Morse-code-like sequence, so one longer clang followed by two quick ones, meant someone must go at once to the meeting point. It was an effective signal that really worked, and any of the nuns could be contacted, immediately, at any time, a sort of medieval mobile phone.

Friday was always the most important day for us. During the week we had to keep an official note of any order marks we had lost, and a total of the marks we had been awarded for our academic work. Every Friday afternoon, there was a very formal ceremony that was called 'Cards'. Each form filed into the hall, with the girl who was top of the class leading the line, while the tiny figure of Reverend Mother was perched precariously on the stage, rather like a general reviewing the troops.

The cards themselves were just flimsy little squares of coloured paper, and were a report on your conduct for that week. Written on them were your name, and your place in the class, but the thing that really mattered, was the paper's colour. Blue was EXCELLENT, pink VERY GOOD and green GOOD, though two of these titles were certainly not what they seemed. 'Excellent' was fine, but 'Very Good' meant that you had lost more than five order marks, which it was very easy to do, and your parents needed to give you a warning about your conduct in school. The green card, 'Good', meant awful, disgraceful, or any other epithet you chose, to describe the week's lack of effort.

Reverend Mother altered her expression to fit the card she was handing out, usually smiling warmly when the colour was blue. Pink often brought a slight shake of the head and raised eyebrows, while she would positively scowl on green, muttering little warnings to suggest that she would soon be talking to your parents about your behavioural problems. Since she had a very strong French accent, and always spoke in a dignified whisper, you were never quite sure what she had actually said, which made the situation very worrying indeed. Rumour had it that there was a white card called 'Indifferent', but none of us had ever seen one and we guessed that any recipient would have been expelled, and so would have disappeared from view.

We all had to wear gloves to receive our cards, a practice that had probably begun when every young lady had a neat white pair for formal occasions, but by the late 1930s, our gloves were primarily to keep our hands warm in cold weather. Very popular at the time were leather 'fur gloves', snugly lined and the backs decorated with rabbit fur. We sat in rows in the school hall, hands clasped on our laps, like aliens from outer space, with strange ape-like furry appendages, issuing from the long sleeves of our white school blouses.

Every week there was another incentive to do well. There were medals to be won! If you were top of your class, you automatically got the silver 'Diligence Medal', shaped like an ornately carved Maltese Cross. The 'Conduct Medal', round, gold, and engraved with a saint's picture, was earned by the simple expedient of not losing one single order mark during the week. That may sound easy but, as one could lose a mark for deportment by slumping in one's chair in class, or a conduct mark for speaking in the corridor between lessons, or one for neatness, by having an untidy desk, it was a very difficult undertaking. Sister Lucy had the 'Music Medal' in her gift. It was silver, oval-shaped, and prettily decorated, and she rarely awarded it, though sometimes someone would win all three medals, and positively clank back to her seat, after Reverend Mother had pinned them on.

In my entire school career, I only won the three medals once, and that was after an unforgettable week of doing all my homework, sitting bolt upright all day at my very tidy desk, and keeping my lips firmly sealed as we lined up in the corridor outside our classroom. My Music Medal was really a gift from Sister Lucy, who had spotted the tremendous effort I was making to be, for once, a good girl, and it certainly did not reflect my efforts at either the piano or the violin, both of which I was learning at the time. Reverend Mother was so surprised she nearly fell off her chair, and muttered something I didn't understand, but took to be a congratulatory remark. Buddy was frankly amazed when I arrived home, decorated like a war hero, but, alas, it never happened again and every Friday, with monotonous regularity, there would be yet another piece of pink paper.

Buddy, who was 'musically challenged', to put it mildly, paid for me to have piano lessons, and as I mastered quite a difficult piece called 'The Rustle of Spring', she mistakenly thought that I had hidden musical talent. This myth was soon exploded when I talked her into letting me learn the violin. At the end of every term, if you had music lessons, you had to play in, what was known as 'the concours', and I had rattled through the 'Rustle of Spring' on the piano, with reasonable success the previous term.

The next concours saw me confidently mounting the stage in the hall, in front of the whole school, clutching my violin, to give a rendering of 'Busy Mill', a tuneless piece, played on open strings. Sister Lucy struck up an accompaniment that aimed to cover my ineptitude, as I raised the bow for the opening notes. At this moment I started to feel terribly nervous and my extended arm began to shake. This made the bow bounce off the strings with a minimum contact, and very little musical sound. Sister Lucy redoubled her efforts, but at no time during my performance did I succeed in getting anything other than the odd squeak out of the violin. I nearly died of embarrassment, and considered fainting on the stage to gain public sympathy, but the agony finally came to an end, as did the violin lessons.

The convent education was, generally, of a very high standard, and I really enjoyed school. All the sisters worked hard, offering each day's teaching to God, so that books never went unmarked, or lessons unprepared, as they did in the real world. Nevertheless, the curriculum certainly restricted our choice of future careers. We did not have lessons in art as it was an 'extra', and though, of course, we studied French as a foreign language, we did not learn German. The only science subject we studied was Physics, which was quite fun, with the very French Sister Flora, explaining the use of salt to clear ice from the roads, as creating a 'free-sing-mick-tcher'. The illustrations in the physics textbook were fascinating. Someone, sitting precariously in one little boat on a lake, banged a gong under the surface, and someone in another boat listened with a submerged giant ear trumpet to the sound, dramatically travelling through the water, in eye-catching wavy lines!

Though the convent had a beautiful garden, there were no science labs in the building, or, for that matter, any domestic science areas. I was genuinely surprised when I went into a state school, to find that there were proper kitchens, where the girls were taught how to cook, and that they made cakes, and iced them at Christmas. In needlework, we only learnt how to darn and do embroidery. Drawn thread work, known as 'broderie anglaise', was very boring. We were each given a piece of cream linen to make a tray cloth, and little by little we pulled out threads going one way, and replaced them with stitches that anchored the threads going the other way, in a decorative pattern. The stitches had to be small and of equal size, and any mistakes meant unpicking and re-doing that particular section.

My poor tray cloth was a grimy grey when, after working on it for two long years, it was finally finished and was taken home to give to Buddy. She seemed to be reasonably impressed, and suggested that we send it to the laundry. They would starch it and restore the colour to cream, so that, hopefully, it would look like new. I can't say whether she was right or not, because the laundry lost it. Two years of my struggles in needlecraft vanished into thin air, and I was extremely upset. Buddy made extensive enquiries, and they offered the maximum compensation for our loss. At six times the cost of laundering, we were paid one and sixpence!

Chapter 2

My favourite subjects at school were English and History taught by one of the small group of English nuns, Sister du Saint Coeur de Marie. We called her 'Sankey', and her lessons were sheer magic, for whether the subject was Shakespeare, parsing and analysis, or the Jacobite Rebellions, it was always fascinating, as she was a superb teacher.

Mrs Cook, who taught us gym, wore a brown tunic, and no-one liked her. She was very fat, and we were unkind enough to be amused that we could see her brown knickers when she leant forward to try to demonstrate some particular gymnastic skill. There was a wind-up gramophone, and we did lots of marching in lines and circles to stirring music like 'Country Gardens', and quite a bit of country dancing. She was particularly keen on highland reels, including something called 'The Sword Dance', in which we jigged about, with arms akimbo, heel-toe pointing over the crossed sticks that served as swords.

We played tennis in the summer and netball in the winter. I had mastered the knack of shooting goals into the net and played 'attack' in the school first team, which made me feel terribly important as I was a year younger than all the others. My real forte, however, was that I actually enjoyed exams, and everything I'd ever heard on the subject would come flooding back into my mind. It was a useful skill.

Outside school, I had been enrolled in the 5th Earlsfield Guide Company, where Peggy was the Company Leader, and she made sure that my GG-trefoil badge was cleaned with Brasso every week, till it shone like gold. She had an impressive show of something called 'All Round

Cords' that meant she had passed every skill test under the sun, and had badges sewn all down both sleeves of her navy cotton uniform, as well as lanyards galore draped around her shoulders. I started off in the Scarlet Pimpernel Patrol, which sounded quite adventurous, and it took a long time before I finally became a patrol leader, and had a lanyard with that symbol of power in the Guides, a whistle. I only ever got one or two badges, like 'Thrift', that was awarded when you opened a Post Office Savings account, and 'Home Nursing', where my experiences as a Matron's daughter made it a very easy option.

In 1934, going to Summer Guide Camp had sounded an attractive idea, especially as Peggy had, by then, joined the Rangers, but a week under canvas was enough to highlight the harsh realities of an outdoor life. It rained a lot, and our ridge tent developed a gentle leak that kept the ground slightly damp, and left an ominous bulge of water on the tent wall near me. The straw palliass was very lumpy, and there was an unending trail of insects keen to join me under my blanket. The cooking was done by a different group every day, but I seemed to spend my week peeling potatoes and washing up unending piles of greasy plates in luke-warm water. I hated the boring food, and, most of all, loathed the trenches that had been dug to act as lavatories. One sat in full view of the other guides, so needless to say, my bowels remained unopened for the entire week!

Of course, there were fun times at camp, and we laughed a lot and learnt how to get on well together. We played games involving a great deal of rushing around, like paper chases, and we went on fairly long treks when you forgot how tired you were by marching in step to chants like:

"LEFT, LEFT, left is the mother of the two fat babies, RIGHT, RIGHT, right in the middle of the kitchen floor!"

and

"LEFT ! LEFT! I had a good home and I left it!"

I especially loved the end of the day, when we all sat around the camp fire, with the glowing, crackling flames lighting the darkness. We would do lots of jolly Guide action songs and rounds, and finally, as the embers started to die, we would stand and salute, singing 'Taps' as the company flag was lowered on the flagpole. Then we would stumble off in the dark, to another uncomfortable night in our tents.

When the week ended, it was wonderful to be back in my own bed at home, dreaming that Franchot Tone, the Hollywood film star I absolutely adored, had come to claim me as his bride. Unfortunately, in the real world, Joan Crawford got there first and snapped him up!

The depression in the economy of the 1930s had not directly affected any of our family, though I remember seeing long queues of the unemployed, outside the local Labour Exchange. They all seemed to be middle-aged, working class men, wearing caps, and looked thoroughly disheartened, as they probably were. Many of them had fought in the First World War, to make a home 'fit for heroes', and returned in 1918 to the reality of unemployment and an existence on the dole, when the short peacetime boom had been followed, in the Twenties, by the traumas of a General Strike, and the Stock Market crash.

Other than my school friends, my social life revolved round an extended 'Higgs' family of uncles, aunts and cousins. Buddy's two brothers were both chemists in the Thames Valley, Stewart having his own pharmacy in Mortlake, and Leonard managing my grandfather's chemist shop in Kingston-upon-Thames. Uncle Stewart and Auntie Gwennie were great fun, and Mortlake was an easy bus ride from Tooting, so we often went there.

Their son, Clive, was about my age, and there was a new addition to the family roughly every seven years, so that Auntie Gwennie always seemed to have a pram to push, which was strangely reassuring. To Clive's enduring annoyance, when he was seven, a little girl was born, who was christened 'Joyce' as she brought such joy to Uncle Stewart, and had golden Shirley Temple curls. Then, seven years after that, another girl, 'Jill' arrived, who inevitably got rather spoilt as the baby of the family. Auntie Gwennie was very musical and always cheerful, except when Clive annoyed her, and then she would chase him round the kitchen table, brandishing a wooden spoon. However, she was quite chubby and he was hyperactive, so she never caught him, but it was a good spectator sport.

The family lived in the large flat over the chemist's shop and Uncle Stewart and Auntie Gwennie called each other 'Moinder', which came from the very romantic 'my own dear', that they had used when they were courting. On our visits there, she would always have made either a delicious jam sponge for tea, or her famous seed cake, from which I had to spend ages taking out the caraway seeds that I hated. We would often go for a walk to see the deer in Richmond Park, or to Sheen Common, to watch Uncle Stewart play bowls, which he took very seriously. Clive and I sometimes went train spotting on the nearby 'wibbly-wobbly bridge', or took fishing nets to a pond, to catch tiddlers which we put in jam jars. Joy vividly remembers lying very still, in case the fish spilt out onto her legs, as Auntie Gwennie pushed the pram home.

The most exciting visit was definitely on the Oxford and Cambridge Boat Race Saturday in the spring, as the finishing line was at Mortlake Brewery, and there were always big crowds on the towpath. We went every year until the war, wearing our dark blue rosettes to support Oxford, and having great fun chanting very loudly:

"Oxford the winner, Cambridge the sinner, put 'em in a matchbox and throw 'em down the river!"

Or

"Oxford downstairs winning all the races, Cambridge upstairs doing up his braces!"

It wasn't at all clear to me why we supported the dark blues, since one of my father's brothers had been at St John's College, Cambridge, but Buddy told us that when she was a little girl, the family horse had always worn an Oxford ribbon, so naturally we must do the same. It never crossed our minds to be turncoats!

When my father had died in 1926, I had been sent to stay for two weeks with Buddy's only sister, Maudie, who was married to Frank Bartle, a dental surgeon. Their lovely house in Surbiton, was just near the river, and the three teenage children, Marjorie, Olive and Bob, led an exciting social life, going to grown-up dances at the Town Hall, and having a succession of pedigree Airedales called 'Bonnie', so it always seemed to be the same dog! Both girls were very talented swimmers, and each, in turn, was a Surrey County Ladies Freestyle Champion, while Olive only narrowly missed selection for the 1936 Olympic Games in Berlin. The family were very well off, and owned a car, a wind-up gramophone and a punt on the river – so I was green with envy.

On the Douglas side, two of my father's three brothers were clergymen in the Church of England. We often went to the Sunday service at their church, St Luke's in Camberwell, usually having lunch with them afterwards. They lived in the vicarage nearby, and they had a cook-housekeeper – the food was usually delicious. I was always terribly impressed by the sight of a huge Stilton cheese, swimming with deep red port, in the centre of the dining table. Uncle Johnny was the vicar and had been made a Canon of Southwark Cathedral, whereas younger, bearded Uncle Charlie was always just the curate. Neither of them ever married, as they firmly believed in the celibacy of the clergy, but they had a wide circle of interesting, influential friends, including Queen Mary, who would occasionally visit Camberwell to plant a tree in the churchyard.

Like my father, who had spoken nine languages, Uncle John was a talented linguist. He spoke seven languages, including Russian and modern Greek, and was in reality an academic, most at ease with either Church leaders or university dons. He often said how much he enjoyed running the boys' clubs at St Luke's, but he was certainly delighted when he was made Chairman of London University, sending us postcards that pictured him in his opulent, ceremonial academic robes.

The Douglas brothers made a very successful team. Uncle Charlie,'C. E.', started a Christian publishing company called 'The Faith Press', with an associated monthly magazine, while Uncle Johnny, 'J.A.', wrote several books about Eastern Orthodox Christianity, and one for children, entitled 'The Home Of Mother Church' St Luke's, in Camberwell, was considered at the time to be a 'slum parish', but the brothers travelled a great deal on the continent, where they were awarded many 'decorations', that ended up hanging on the wall in the study at the vicarage.

By a strange coincidence, when the war came, they were evacuated to East Sheen, where they ran the church that Uncle Stewart's family attended, then, finally, they were rewarded with a famous London church, St Michael and All Angels in the City. I recently looked them up on Google and there is a great deal about their careers. On Wikipedia there are portraits of both of them, but, bizarrely, the supposed picture of 'C.E.' is actually one of Uncle John, while the 'J.A.' portrait is of a clergyman I have never seen before in my life!

My father's only sister, Auntie Mary, who had been presented at court in Queen Victoria's reign, was terribly grand, and had married a colonel in the Indian Army. She had very aristocratic friends and I would be sent to stay with her, either at Ickenham, where their retirement bungalow was called 'Sarawak', after the country where Uncle George had been an army commander, or in the Isle of Wight, where her daughter, Cousin Kitty, was married to an ex-army officer rejoicing under the name of Captain Cook.

During my visit to Ickenham in August, 1935, the official announcement was made that Lady Alice Montague Douglas Scott, the daughter of the Duke of Buccleugh, was engaged, and Auntie Mary was terribly excited. "My cousin is going to marry The Duke of Gloucester!", she announced. It dawned on me that if it was my aunt's cousin, it must be my cousin too, but I didn't think to ask for details about our connection with the Buccleughs. When I mentioned at school that one of my relatives was joining the royal family, no-one believed me, particularly when we didn't get invited to the wedding!

By 1936, when the King abdicated in order to marry Wallis Simpson, the British Dental Hospital had closed and Buddy had become the Matron at St Benedict's Nursing Home in Nightingale Lane, Clapham South. The post was not residential, so we had moved from Tooting, into a flat just near Wandsworth Common. I was about to leave school, and had passed Senior Oxford, with exemption from Matric, but it would have been much too expensive for Buddy to send me to university, so there had to be another plan.

She had heard of a London agency called 'Gabbitas and Thring', which specialised in temporary posts for well-educated school leavers, offering, in effect, a gap year, before starting a career in the real world. In return for acting as assistant teachers or assistant matrons, young ladies could spend a year, earning pocket money and having lessons in art and music in expensive prep schools. It could have been called, "Working Your Way Through Finishing School"! My application was accepted, and I was duly packed off to Buckinghamshire at the beginning of the new September term.

Chapter 3

Woodlands School, Great Missenden, in leafy, stockbroker belt Buckinghamshire, was an expensive prep school, used by ex-pats from all over the world, to give their children the benefit of a socially acceptable start to their education in the UK. In addition to qualified staff, they employed three young ladies as 'assistants'. I was the only assistant teacher, but there were two assistant matrons, both from very up-market families, and much more worldly-wise than I was.

We shared an annex in the school grounds and Margot, whose family owned an amusement park in Margate, was very attractive and great fun. She had two brothers, so she knew, by hearsay, what were euphemistically called "the facts of life". Naturally, she passed the information on to me at the earliest opportunity. I already knew where babies came from, as we had several medical books at home, with diagrams of foetuses in various stages of growth, but I had absolutely no idea how they got there, or how they could, finally, get out. Sex education, needless to say, had not been part of the curriculum at the convent, and, surprisingly, we certainly never discussed it between ourselves. It would probably have been the sin of 'having impure thoughts' and we would have had to tell the priest at our next confession. Margot's description of what happened was not attractive. It sounded very intrusive and not remotely desirable, and I certainly couldn't see myself agreeing to take part in any such activity!

I slightly wondered why Buddy hadn't said anything about the topic when I went away from home, but, doubtless, she thought I knew it all, already. She had once mentioned that passionate fathers produced female children, and, as she had had three girls, (another sister, Betty, had died seven months before I was born), this seemed to mean something about my father. She had also remarked that the very popular Prince of Wales could not have children, as he had fallen off his rocking horse when he was a little boy. The connection puzzled me, but I made a mental note to keep any children I might ever have, well away from rocking horses.

My duties, as assistant teacher at Woodlands School, were undemanding. I helped with the five year olds, under the guidance of a very pleasant, qualified Froebel teacher. I mixed paints for their efforts at art, sang along with them in music lessons and played with them or comforted them, as circumstances required. I liked being called 'Miss Douglas', for even in the staff room teachers rarely used Christian names to each other, though, of course, Margot called me 'Dougie', as everyone always had at school. The year went by like a shot.

When my time at Woodlands was over, there had still been no decision about my future career. Then someone told Buddy, that the Civil Service offered excellent opportunities for school leavers who had, what was then called, 'School Certificate'. Entry was by competitive examination, and all that needed to be done, was to chose which post to apply for, and take the necessary test. The lowest grade was clerical assistant, and as Buddy had absolutely no idea what people did in offices, that seemed the best option. The exam was not difficult, just basic English and Maths, so it was hardly a surprise that I passed with flying colours. All that I had to do now was wait to be posted to a particular government department, so that my new career as a civil servant could start.

The letter arrived at the flat in Wandsworth Common, only a few days after we got the result of the exam. It offered a position on the staff of the Receiver for the Metropolitan Police District, in New Scotland Yard, and, the following week, I should report to the Engineers' Department. The letter pointed out that, unlike posts in one of the various ministries, there would be no opportunity to transfer to a different area of administration once I had joined the Receiver's Office, but I promptly wrote and accepted the offer. Buddy was delighted. "My daughter works in New Scotland Yard", sounded very impressive, and she was pleased to hear that the post carried a non-contributory pension at sixty. When the reality of the appointment sank in, I started to worry. What use could I possibly be to an Engineers' Department?

Tossing and turning in bed that night, the answer came to me. It was obvious. The department needed someone to watch the boilers, and I would be keeping a constant check on the temperature gauges, to make sure they didn't explode. There could be no other reason for employing someone like me in engineering. I just hoped that the boiler room wouldn't be too hot, as it was August. I was so totally convinced that I knew what was going to happen that, when I reported to New Scotland Yard the following Wednesday, I was amazed that the lift went up, and not down.

The Engineers' Department was on the top floor, in the left hand turret of the wonderful building facing the Thames. It was a huge open plan office, with a glass partition providing a separate space for the head of the department, who was a cheerful, kindly man of about fifty, slightly balding, a little plump, but very smartly dressed, and he explained what my work involved. I was to keep a ledger. It sounded impressive, but I had no idea what it meant.

The main office, he said, was divided into sections, each one having a clerical officer in charge, and he made it clear that this ledger was very important. I must work with great care, checking police car petrol and mileage forms and accurately recording them. Every car, it seemed, had a number, and the whole system would break down if the proper checks weren't made. I trembled at the thought of this tremendous responsibility, and hoped that I did not bring the entire Metropolitan Police fleet of cars to a juddering halt. The head of the department then introduced me to his deputy, who would take me to meet my immediate boss, the section leader.

When we went into the main office I was very impressed. There were huge filing cabinets, great big tables and lots of chairs. Everyone seemed to be working very hard, and, sitting at each table, were two or three people. To my total amazement, they were all MEN and they were all quite young! My section leader was very handsome, tall and fair, with pink cheeks, blue eyes and beautifully aquiline features. They called him Norrie. He patiently showed me just what to do, and clearly took his responsibilities very seriously.

The minute the deputy head of the department left the office, all hell broke loose. A barrage of paper clips was flicked through the air and an atmosphere of light-hearted fun took over. One by one, they came over to welcome me. There was Lofty, whose real name was Neville, and who looked just like Noel Coward; Jamie, with tousled curly hair and a rich Scottish accent; Arthur, the short, chubby one; 'Dead', (his surname was Deadman), slim and athletic, and Stan, who was a bit older than the others, and the only one who wasn't a bachelor. With Norrie, it made seven young chaps, and I was the only girl. I was seventeen and totally overcome.

Of course I fell in love, starting with Lofty. He was about thirty, wonderfully sophisticated and witty, and clearly had an exciting social life, somewhere in the Thames Valley, in a world of tennis parties and punts on the river. Of course he didn't return my feelings, so I was careful to keep them to myself, though the others guessed and gently teased me. I told Buddy how wonderful he was, but she didn't take me seriously enough to ask where he had gone to school, which would have been her first question about a potential future son-in-law.

Next was Jamie, of the tousled hair. He was a member of a territorial army regiment called 'The London Scottish', and talked a lot about drinking binges with the lads, so that even I could see why he was still a bachelor in his mid-thirties. Yet I dragged Buddy off to watch him march down The Mall with his regiment, in full kilt and sporran, to the swirl of the bagpipes. I thought he looked adorable, and Buddy quite warmed to the idea of meeting him, but it never happened.

Every day in the office, from 10 till 5, was a delight. I loved the way the men joked with each other, and the much gentler teasing they reserved for me. I had never had the pleasure of young men friends before, and I really enjoyed the time I spent with them. They treated me very kindly, as they would have done a puppy, recognising that I was only an innocent seventeen year old, straight out of a girls' convent school They all flirted outrageously, giving me little hugs that made me thoroughly enjoy male company. It was a boost to my confidence, for which I have been grateful all my life.

The actual 'work' was considerably less exciting. Keeping a ledger, turned out to be as dull as ditchwater. There were piles of invoices, renewed daily, and I had to find the right page in the big ledger and copy down the information from each one. Then I had to file the invoice in the right cabinet, in the right drawer, in the right folder. I was not a natural filing clerk, and, but for the fun going on around me, with jolly chatter and flying paper clips, it would soon have become very, very boring work indeed.

On the same floor as the main turret office, there were several rooms where small groups dealt with different aspects of the Engineering Department's work. There was the usual typing pool full, I noted enviously, of attractive, smartly dressed girls in their mid-twenties. Sometimes they would venture into the main office and could always be sure of a very warm welcome. Once they had gone out of the room, there would be the usual ribbing of one of the bachelors, including Norrie, my section leader, who was suspected of fancying a particularly sophisticated secretary. He would blush and bury himself in his work, until the chatter passed on to a new topic.

Norrie was a very serious chap, extremely keen on cricket, and always immaculately dressed. He did not flick paper clips at the others, so I thought he wasn't quite as much fun, but he was very handsome and, when he smoked his pipe, he looked rather like a picture on a knitting pattern. I think he found my ledger-keeping rather exasperating, as I kept inventing new, quicker ways of putting invoices into the filing cabinets. This usually meant that they landed up in the wrong drawer and it took hours for him to find them when they were needed to answer a query.

One day, chatting to him in the office, I casually mentioned that I was going to Regent's Park that evening, to see Shakespeare's 'A Midsummer Night's Dream'. It turned out that he was going there too, on his own. As, clearly, we both loved the theatre and Shakespeare, he suggested that we could meet at the box office in the park, and sit together to watch the play.

It was a warm evening in early June, and Norrie was already in the box office queue when I arrived, so I joined him and he suggested that he could take my money and get the ticket. We took our seats on the folding, green metal chairs about five rows from the front, as the notes of the wonderful Mendelssohn overture came softly from the speakers high up in the trees. The floodlights attracted a bevy of fluttering moths, and the magic of Shakespeare's play held us entranced. It was an evening I shall never forget.

After the play ended, Norrie suggested that we walk to 'The Strand Arcade' and have a milk shake, so we made our way there, talking about the performances in the play we had just seen, and other productions we had enjoyed. It turned out that our tastes were very similar. The Milk Bar in the arcade was quite busy, but Norrie ordered two chocolate shakes and a slice each of datey-raisin cake, which was delicious. Not wanting to be a financial burden, I offered to pay my share of the bill, a suggestion he considered for a moment, before declining quite graciously, saying that I could pay, next time!

In fact, the 'next time' turned out to be a proper date. He asked me if I would like to go, one evening, for a trip down the Thames to Greenwich, to see the famous Observatory. The little steamers left from The Embankment, just outside our office, and we could catch the five-thirty sailing, the following Wednesday, if I was free. I accepted at once, and hurried home to give the good news to Buddy. Of course she asked where Norrie had gone to school, and I knew the answer. It was called 'St Olave's and St Saviour's', a grammar school at Tower Bridge, and he played cricket for 'The Old Olavians' every Saturday. Then she wondered what his father did, and I had absolutely no idea.

The following Wednesday was warm and sunny, a perfect early July evening for a trip on the Thames. We had seats on the upper deck and I thought how wonderful London looked from the river. Norrie had bought me a little box of chocolates, 'Cadbury's Milk Tray', so we munched them as the steamer chugged its way to Greenwich. He checked the time of the return journey to Westminster, and we set off, through the park, and up to the Observatory building at the top of the hill. I hadn't realised how important Greenwich was for the setting of clocks all over the world, and all the technical equipment looked terribly impressive. Then the evening got extremely interesting. We sat on a bench in the park and talked, and he put an arm round me and kissed me. A shot of electricity ran up my arm, and, in that instant, I knew that having Norrie as a boy friend, was going to be great fun, whatever his father did!

Dusk was beginning to fall as we made our way, hand in hand, back to the quay, and it was a little disconcerting to see our steamer chugging away on its return voyage to Westminster. We had missed the boat. Such was the romantic haze that surrounded us, that we accepted the situation quite philosophically. I expected us to catch a bus, but Norrie was adamant, it would be a pleasant stroll, through attractive streets, so we would walk back. Such was the effect of 'Cloud Nine' that I didn't put forward any objection to the idea, and, hand in hand, that is just what we did.

Oh, it was such a long way, and the route took us along dreary streets, past mean little houses, with dustbins by their front doors. By the time we reached the nearest tube station, I was really exhausted, so when we said our goodbyes, I told him that I had had a great time, though, maybe, it might have been easier to have taken a bus back. To my surprise he agreed and it turned out that we had walked because he hadn't brought enough money to pay the unexpected return fare!

Of course sharp eyes in the Engineers' Office soon spotted the budding romance in their midst, and Norrie was given a lot of affectionate teasing, as a rather off-beat Romeo.. I had been moved, much to my annoyance, to one of the side offices, to widen my experience of the work of the department, where the section leader was an old chap everyone called, 'Pa', and who smoked a foul-smelling pipe all day. It was just a different ledger, this time checking on spare parts and the police garages. There was a large station-style clock on the wall and I used to look at the time and determine not to look again, until I felt ten minutes had passed. It was a sort of game to assuage my boredom. Without fail, about three or four minutes had gone, by the time I checked, so I felt I was wishing my life away. I simply did not like the work, and started considering other career choices. In a way, the outbreak of war saved me.

Chapter 4

1938 ended well, in the world outside. Neville Chamberlain's return from Munich, waving bits of paper had, we all thought, sorted out 'Adolf', that Charlie Chaplin-like, gesticulating, German dictator. The threat of war, that had led to nearly everyone I knew volunteering for some kind of national service, seemed to have passed, and we looked back on the gloomy news, and the anxious filling of sandbags, as little hiccups in the smooth passage of our young lives. Norrie, and several others, including my sister Peggy's husband, Dick, had joined the Territorial Army, and, not to be outdone, I became a member of the British Red Cross Society, which was quite easy, as Buddy was the local commandant. We all went on short training initiations, the men to weekend army camps, and I had a two day spell in a local hospital.

The summer had deepened my fondness for Norrie, (now known by his Christian name as 'Ernest'), and I had become the archetypal girl friend, dutifully spending almost every summer weekend watching him play cricket. (I was secretly very relieved that he didn't play any team games in the winter!) He had gone on a summer cricket tour in Devon, with the Old Olavians, and he took cricket very seriously, for, though he was not a natural athlete, as an opening batsman, he could stone-wall as well as anyone. I enjoyed his company, and when the cricket season ended, at weekends we went to the theatre, the cinema, and on one awful occasion, to watch Millwall play football at The Den. It was not a pretty sight! Buddy had met Ernest and was pleased that he smoked a pipe, (which she thought was a very manly thing to do), and I had gone to tea with his parents. His father was involved with printing in some way, and I could see that Ernest was the apple of his mother's eye.

I did still have other interests, like Jack, who worked in another office at the Yard, and made me laugh. He had been educated at Christ's Hospital, having won a major scholarship when he was only eleven. He was very clever and played the violin, which I knew from my struggles at school, was not an easy thing to do.

Buddy and I had decided to spend Christmas 1938 at a hotel in Brighton, and when Ernest heard about it, he asked if he could join us. I was delighted, and we had a wonderful time playing the games the proprietors had organised, and eating absolutely delicious food, with no washing-up to follow.

Our prospects for 1939 looked rosy. To my slight surprise, Buddy raised no objections when we planned a week's holiday in Belgium without her. It was a real bargain, a week in a hotel in early June, in the seaside resort of Blankenberg, costing only £6.10s, for half board and the return journey by coach and ferry from Victoria, and looked too good to miss. Of course we would have separate rooms, which went without saying, and the pictures of the hotel were suitably impressive. It was a first visit to the Continent for both of us and when we applied for our passports, we felt like seasoned travellers. Little did we know that war was about to make such holidays impossible for a long time to come.

We had wonderful weather. I persuaded Ernest to try riding on the lovely sandy beach, and the horses were, as I had promised, very quiet and well-behaved. We hired bicycles and went for long tours of the very flat hinterland, and took a coach trip to the beautiful city of Bruges, where he was able to buy his favourite pipe tobacco, called 'Balkan Sobranie', quite cheaply. I didn't smoke, so I bought two miniature bottles of brandy for Buddy. The week went by very quickly.

When we got back to the office there were lots of questions about our holiday, and I suddenly realised that everyone thought we must have had a VERY romantic time! It had actually never occurred to me, (though I can't speak for Ernest), that we might sleep together. It just wasn't done. We weren't married.

As the summer progressed the spectre of war once again raised its ugly head. This time it was a threat to Poland, a country far away, about which we knew absolutely nothing. We saw pictures in the paper of a triumphant Hitler, surrounded by swastika flags and cheering crowds, and of elderly politicians in England, who already looked overwhelmed by an approaching catastrophe.

We heard the declaration of war on the radio, just as Buddy and I were about to go for a bike ride, and we were actually cycling by Wandsworth Common when the first siren went. It was a dramatic moment as we had no idea what to expect. Was it the gas attack we had been threatened with? Would the bombers come across the sky and destroy London? Actually, it was a false alarm and we hurried safely back home, but we realised that we now lived in a different world.

The immediate reaction of the government was to call-up the Territorial Army. Within days Ernest, in the artillery, got orders to report to his HQ and he was assigned to The Royal Devon Yeomanry, to be instructed in the use of twenty-five pounder guns. He never found out why he was posted to a west country regiment, as the only contact he had ever had with Devon was the previous year's cricket tour, but he got his rail pass and set off for Exeter. Several others from the office disappeared. Jamie and the London Scottish, were in the first wave of the army to travel to France, and there was an excitement in the air. The older generation remembered the First World War, and there was a cheerful certainty that Germany would be beaten yet again, as it had been in 1918.

It was soon clear that there was nothing like a war to bring out the latent patriotism of the British, Everybody seemed to be volunteering for something. The Army, the Navy and the RAF, called for men and women in the right age groups, but the country also needed air raid wardens, fire fighters, nurses for the first aid posts and a whole host of other vital personnel, for what was called, 'The War Effort'. Slogans like 'Dig For Victory', resulted in an amazing wielding of spades and forks in their gardens, by people who had previously never even given a thought to where vegetables came from, when they bought them at their local greengrocer's.

Local parks got dug up, and a 'Land Army' of young women was recruited to help on farms all over the country, where the men folk had gone into the forces. We held our breath and waited for Hitler to launch an air attack on us, as he had everywhere else, but nothing happened. The British Expeditionary Force, made up of regiments of the regular army, set sail for France, taking the traditional ferry route, through Folkestone and Dover, to Boulogne and Calais. The Naval and Air Force Reserves were called into action, and everyone carried their gas mask wherever they went. Hundreds of children were evacuated from the big cities into towns and villages in the country. Bewildered and labelled, they were packed into trains to travel to supposed safety, as weeping parents watched the steam engines pulling away from station platforms. I was very glad that I wasn't one of them!

The Receiver's Office staff were also evacuated, but to Wimbledon, to a large house with a beautiful garden. There was a big change in personnel, as many of the younger staff had been called up. My status had changed, too. I was engaged. Ernest had asked me to marry him when the war was over. He thought he might be sent overseas, and he wanted me to promise that I would be there, waiting, when he got back We were actually on a bus at the time, and I agreed, so we went on to buy the ring that would tell the world I was spoken for.

I had never been a great lover of jewellery; I always seemed to lose the things I had, but it was very exciting choosing an engagement ring. My July birthstone is a ruby, so I picked a simple square cut one, with a small diamond set on either side. I remember it cost five pounds, which seemed an awful lot of money at the time. We got it at a shop, which had, as an advertising joke: "If someone says, 'I'll give you a ring', just answer, 'Make it a Bravington!'", and we did. Buddy thought I was far too young to make a commitment to marry anyone, but she reluctantly gave her permission and the official announcement was duly made.

Once his artillery training was completed, Ernest was given a week of embarkation leave, and then would be going across the Channel to be ready to take on the invaders, if and when they arrived. It was a dreadful thought that, at only barely twenty, he might be injured, or even killed.

We tried to stay optimistic and hope that the war would not last long, but our parents remembered, all too well, what had happened in 1914. He promised to write as soon as the army allowed him to, and to come back at the earliest opportunity in one piece. I kept a cheerful smile and went to wave him goodbye at Waterloo Station, when he rejoined his unit.

It was not a successful farewell gesture. Trying to be helpful, I slammed the carriage door, not realising that Ernest's new sergeant-major had his fingers in the door frame. He was big strong man, but his face drained of colour as we desperately tried to get the carriage door open, to release his fingers. He was muttering several words that, possibly fortunately, I couldn't quite make out. When his hand was free, it was clear that it had been damaged, but I never heard exactly how. It was not the best start to Ernest's life in the artillery!

It was, however, definitely a day to remember, for quite unknown to us, when we arrived at Waterloo, we had had our picture taken by a roving newspaper photographer. It was a view, from the back, of Ernest carrying his kitbag with his name and, (slightly like a post code), his number, 897035, clearly visible, in big white script. I had my hand out, grasping the rope at the top, and the caption read," Her soldier sweetheart had to go back after a few days leave, so she saw him off in a practical way, by giving him a helping hand with his kitbag.". Someone spotted it in the paper the next day, and it caused a great deal of amusement among our friends.

Buddy, as a trained nurse and a Red Cross Commandant, was soon called up, too. She was to be a QA. The Queen Alexandra's Nursing Service, composed entirely of qualified SRNs, was the official army nursing organisation. The Red Cross and the St John's Ambulance Brigade, formed the Voluntary Aid Detachment, the VAD, which was for unqualified amateurs, like me. They were also expecting to provide extra staff for hard-pressed civilian hospitals, if and when the feared rush of air raid casualties came. This was called the 'Civil Nursing Reserve'. I had done my initial 48 hour training, and as there were no injured soldiers, I expected to be called into the CNR when help was needed.

Buddy had gone to be a QA in Surrey, so I moved to a flat, nearer to Wimbledon and the office. I shared it with a colleague called Beryl, who had an exasperating habit of unselfish forgiveness that nearly drove me mad. She was so kind and considerate, that I almost longed for my sister's tetchy moodiness, which was definitely saying something. Beryl really was a very nice girl, a devout Baptist, and a keen worker at her local chapel.

She took me to watch an adult baptism, which I found strangely worrying, as it seemed such an extreme version of 'the baby and the font', that I was used to, as a Catholic. The pool in which the appellants were totally immersed was very modern, but the ceremonial ducking of fully-clothed adults, looked spectacularly medieval. I couldn't help remembering tales of the tests for witchcraft, but there was no doubting the sincerity of everyone involved, so I felt very mean having such uncharitable thoughts.

Later, when Beryl asked how I felt about adult baptism, I commented on the huge differences in the actual ceremony between the branches of the Christian church, but she reminded me that the gospels told us that 'In my father's house are many mansions', so I didn't say any more about it. Afterwards we were offered tea and lemonade, and that was also pretty different from the champagne I had enjoyed at various family Church of England christenings before the war.

I probably stretched Beryl's patience to its limit. There was something challenging about her determination never to get annoyed, that brought out the worst in me. I just wanted her to disagree about something. Anything. I hated the maxim, 'a soft answer turneth away wrath', and I was quite unused to the 'turn the other cheek' mentality.

To my shame, I went to ridiculous lengths to get her to react irritably. I very nearly succeeded one evening, when she had laid out a whole lot of photographs on the dining room table. She had taken quite a lot of time to arrange them carefully, in the right order, and was just about to put them, neatly, into an album. We also used the table, covered with what was called an ironing blanket, for pressing our clothes. I looked at the pictures and said, "Oh, Beryl, do you need the table? I was going to do my ironing?" There was a second's pause and the tiniest of gasps, then she quickly gathered everything up, saying, "Of course you can have the table. I can do the photos later." I remember feeling terribly guilty, and had to find some ironing to do.

Despite prophesies of gloom and doom, not a lot was happening in the suburbs of London, where I was living. The newspapers called it 'The Phoney War', because there had been no German invasion of France and Belgium, as older people remembered in 1914, and there had been no bombing, as yet, of cities and vulnerable civilians in Britain. What Hitler's game plan was, we had no idea. Some of the city children who had been evacuated started to drift back, welcomed home, enthusiastically, by relieved families.

Of course, the rationing of food that started in January, 1940, was a nasty shock. Butter and sugar, two of the things I would have thought vital to my life, were the first to catch the attention of the new Ministry of Food. Butter could, at a push, be replaced by margarine, but sugar was irreplaceable. I hated saccharine, which gave a bitter edge to my favourite cups of tea or coffee, so I had to stop taking sugar in one or the other. I tried tea first, as Buddy always said that sugar spoiled the taste, but she was quite wrong. Sugarless tea was horrid, so I tried sugarless coffee. Much better. However, even with using it only in tea, there were other demands on the magic of sugar.

If we stewed fruit, it had to be sweetened, and so honey was in great demand. If we made a pudding, golden syrup was wonderful, but quickly disappeared from the shops. Later, when jam was rationed, and, of course, sweets of all kinds, it was very difficult if, like me, you had a sweet tooth. Somehow rationing crept up on us. Foodstuffs had ration books and petrol and clothing had coupons, which became currency in the hands of the spivs on the black market. The tiny piece of meat we got, made a Sunday roast a thing of the past, and many luxuries, like whisky and tobacco, were soon in short supply. It already seemed like a siege economy.

Buddy had been released from the QA's, in February, 1940, as she was one of their oldest volunteers, and the army hospital was over-staffed. She decided to take a non-resident post, as a district nurse in the north London suburb of Enfield, where she could buy her own house, ready for her retirement, once the war was over. It was really exciting, joining her in the search for somewhere that she could afford, in a good location.

We found a pretty terrace, in a little road, aptly named Florence Avenue, with the railway station for Kings Cross, just across Windmill Hill, the main road. The house had a very attractive arched doorway, three double bedrooms, two good reception rooms and a large kitchen, complete with a scullery that had a door onto the long garden. There would be lots of room for both of us, and for Ernest, too, when we got married. I loved the house, which had a big cherry tree in the back garden, so, leaving Beryl to find a less demanding flatmate, I moved back to sharing with Buddy.

Chapter 5

Late spring in 1940, brought an abrupt end to the phoney war. In France, in May the German blitzkrieg struck, in a pincer movement, sweeping all before it, towards the Channel coast. Ernest and Dick, Peggy's husband, were both in the army in France, and the radio told us that the British forces were retreating in the direction of Calais. It was hoped to rescue at least some of them, before the German tanks arrived.

They were terribly anxious days. On May 10th a new Prime Minister, Winston Churchill, led the country, and 'Operation Dynamo' was put into action from Dover Castle. The papers showed pictures of little boats joining the Royal Navy, in a desperate attempt to reach the troops who had arrived in Dunkirk. There were shots of the ships, and the long queues of soldiers, patiently waiting on the beach, being attacked by German planes. The courage of the sailors and their stricken comrades in the army, moved us all to tears, and it still does, seventy years later. We thanked God for saving some of the defeated army, and hoped and prayed that our two special soldiers would make it back home.

The days went by, and there was no news. Others heard from their friends, but neither Peggy, nor I, had any idea what had happened to Dick and Ernest. We feared that they may not have survived the dangers that had overtaken them. Then, out of the blue, in Florence Avenue, the phone rang. It was Ernest, safely back in England, having been rescued from the Dunkirk beaches by a cross-channel ferry. He never forgot my immediate reaction, when, totally amazed, I cried, "I thought you were dead!" He was to be given several days leave to recover from the ordeal, and would be in Enfield by the end of the week. I was overjoyed.

Finally, Peggy heard that Dick had been much less fortunate. His unit, given the responsibility of supplying vital drinking water to the exhausted stragglers heading for the coast, was surrounded by German tanks, and surrendered at gun point. They were then transported, on foot and by rail, to be prisoners of war in Poland. I had really liked Dick, who was a talented architect, and enjoyed playing cards. He had got on well with Ernest, and we were very relieved that he was alive, though very sad that he was a prisoner of war.

It later emerged that, during part of the journey to the Polish prison camp, Dick had been accidentally knocked down by a German motorcyclist. The severity of his injury was not fully realised for some time, but increasing back pain resulted in an X-ray, which showed he had developed a tubercular abscess at the base of his spine. He was hospitalised and treated, but graded as a future non-combatant, he was repatriated three years later, via Switzerland, in a spinal carriage.

In June, 1940, the main cause for rejoicing was that Ernest was home and Dick was alive. Not everyone was so lucky, and it was heartbreaking to hear that the genial, rugby-playing only son of the head of the Engineers' Office, had bled to death in a ditch on the retreat to Calais. The war was already causing terrible distress, and it had only just begun. The success of the Germans in France, made it inevitable that they would now turn to the task of invading England. Just quite how, nobody knew, but an attack from the air seemed the obvious preliminary, and hospitals around the big cities, especially London, were put on red alert. Ernest had been posted to Northern Ireland, following his return from Dunkirk, and I was really pleased to be called up by the Civil Nursing Reserve, while I was still only nineteen.

My posting was to 'The West Middlesex Hospital', in Twickenham, in the Thames Valley. It wasn't too far away from Enfield, so that I could see Buddy if I had a day off, and, like everyone else, I wanted to do my bit for the war effort. Living in a hospital would be no problem. I had spent several years in one, as the Matron's daughter, and I was confident that I could do useful work as a nurse. I went to the London outfitters for my Red Cross uniform, and was measured for a navy outdoor coat and little round hat, blue cotton dresses and white aprons with a large red cross on the front, white muslin squares for 'butterfly' caps and a very attractive navy cloak, lined with scarlet, for wearing off the ward.

Under Buddy's strict eye, I bought a watch with a seconds hand to take pulses, and an expensive pair of surgical scissors to keep in the special pocket in the blue dress. I knew that very comfortable shoes were a must, as I had not forgotten the agony of burning feet when I did my 48 hour training, and, just like school, I had black woollen stockings. Ernest was delighted that I was joining him in His Majesty's Forces, and very nicely said how lucky he thought my future patients would be, to have such a wonderful nurse. I was ready for action.

Through the post, I got a warrant to travel to Twickenham on the train, and, to my surprise, I was to go First Class. It seemed that the VAD were considered to be officers, which was really quite funny, in view of the bedpan duties we were to undertake on the wards. I dressed carefully in my smart new uniform, though I felt that the little round hat wasn't quite what I would have chosen, and Buddy gave me her sweet ration, in case I got hungry on the journey. We went over the road to the main line railway station and I caught the steam train to King's Cross, taking a first class carriage and leaving Buddy rather forlornly waving on the empty platform. It was a big adventure into the unknown.

The West Middlesex was quite a modern hospital that had been built in the early thirties, and was in a road with a lot of fairly new semi-detached houses. I reported to Reception, and was taken to meet one of the senior ward sisters who had been put in charge of the VAD contingent. She explained that I was to start on the men's surgical ward, on day duty from 8am to 8pm. I would be given two hours off each day, and a day off every week, as long as there was not a state of emergency. Sister said that I was to be billeted in one of the houses along the road, as there was no space in the hospital's own nurses' quarters, and gave me an address on a piece of paper, suggesting that I go there straight away. It wasn't quite what I'd expected, but I picked up my suitcase and went down the hospital drive, and along the road, to find my new home.

The house looked exactly like all the other semis, with a neat front garden and white net curtains in the window. I rang the bell and the door opened to disclose the huge form of Mrs G. She was quite young, but I had never seen anyone so fat. She filled the doorway, so that I couldn't see past her into the hall. She told me later that, before she had had her little boy, she had been quite slim, and the wedding photo on the dining room sideboard, certainly confirmed this. Mrs G always gave a very dramatic description of the tremendous weight she had gained in a few months, with the phrase, "Who would have thought that the human skin would stretch that far?" Certainly not me.

My room was the upstairs back bedroom, modestly furnished with a double bed, covered by a satiny pink bedspread, plus a wardrobe and a chest of drawers, in dark varnished wood. There was a bedside table, with a bedside lamp, an upright chair, and plain blackout curtains. She warned me that the air raid wardens were very hot on spotting even a chink of light, and I must close the curtains carefully, once it got dark outside. She then took me into the back garden to see the Anderson shelter, where we all had to go if the sirens sounded. The entrance, down three concrete steps, seemed very small, and the main structure, made of corrugated metal, covered in lumps of earth to give protection against bomb blast, looked too small to house Mrs G, never mind the rest of us. I made a mental note to stay in bed and avoid the crush.

Life in the Civil Nursing Reserve was slightly unsatisfactory. The VADs did not fit into any category that the hospital hierarchy recognised. We were temporary, and though untrained, we were not really like the probationers, who saw nursing as a permanent career. I was very young, but some VADs were in their thirties, and had set attitudes that they found difficult to change. Some had held responsible jobs before the war which had paid well, and they were shocked to find how little money they now earned. I had two huge advantages in that I was young and excited by the challenge of being 'in the forces', but secondly that I already, thanks to Buddy, understood how the strict protocol of life in hospital worked.

I was always careful to recognise that the ward sister's word was law, and at no time, offered an opinion on how anything should be done. I never tried to speak to the doctors, however dishy I thought they were, or complain about something I had been given to do. Keeping your head down, and working hard, had been drummed into me since I was seven. It was tempting to suggest a change in any procedure, when it was apparent that it was a waste of time, but it was an unwise thing to do.

The patients on the men's surgical ward were not the handsome young soldiers I had hoped for, with romantic wounds that I could gently tend as they watched my skilful fingers work their magic. In the main they were pensioners, in their sixties and seventies, touchy and ungrateful, greeting their apparently dreary wives at visiting times, with complaints about hospital food and being woken at six every morning. Many of them had prostate trouble which, at that time, involved a demoralising two stage operation, and they resented the days they were spending in a hospital ward. I fell back on being cheerful, but always too busy to listen to their pet moans. On the whole it worked, though carrying innumerable 'bottles', discretely disguised under white cloths, in response to cries of "Nurse! Nurse! Can I have a bottle?" did seem rather a doubtful contribution to the war effort.

The daily routine of bed-making, (with the 'hospital corners' Buddy had always insisted on at home), giving blanket baths, doing 'backs' for bedridden patients, that involved an alcohol rub and a dusting of talcum to prevent bedsores, distributing meals onto bed-tables and clearing everything back into the ward kitchen, giving out bedpans, taking and recording pulses and temperatures, and so on, kept us occupied and time went very quickly. Ward-maids did the main cleaning, but patients' lockers were our responsibility, and it was a constant struggle to keep them tidy, especially when the bunches of grapes had been half eaten, and the remains of a cake put crumbs everywhere.

The two vital rounds of the day were Matron's, when everything had to be perfect, and the Consultant's, when sister would send us into the sluice to clean bedpans, lest we get in the way of the king of the hospital world. The end of normal life at the West Middlesex came in the first week of September,1940, with the Blitz. The ear-spitting wail of air raid sirens, meant that German bombers were on their way to London, We were on full red alert.

Ridiculously, none of us were afraid for our own lives. We never even considered that we might get killed or injured, as we tried to deal with the terrible results of the bombing. The ambulance crews brought in a steady stream of bodies. Men, women and children, all given an awful similarity by the thick layers of brick dust that covered their hands and faces. Doctors, in a brief examination, declared them dead or alive, and any corpses were immediately sent to the mortuary to be identified. The living were laid on beds in our reception ward, and unqualified staff like me, were directed to gently wash their faces, and if they were conscious, reassure them that all would be well. They were safe.

It was the end of any time off duty, and the day staff worked well into the night to try to cope with the huge numbers of casualties. As we ran out of space, mattresses were put on the floor between beds, and anyone who could walk was treated and discharged. I shall never forget the sight of an ambulance man carrying the body of a boy of about seven or eight, whose sturdy little legs, in knee length grey socks, dangled loosely down. The sight of children dying, upset everyone, but we had to put our anger and grief aside to help the rest of the injured. Once our hospital had absolutely no space left, casualties were diverted to other places, often miles away, and only then could real treatment of our admissions begin.

Mr T had been standing with his back to the fire in his sitting room, while his wife was sheltering in the cupboard under the stairs, when the bomb exploded. The blast brought the ceiling down, and he was pinned onto the open fire by the debris. Mrs T had a broken leg, but he suffered extensive third degree burns of his back, from mid-thigh up to the shoulder blade. The firemen put the fire out and he was taken to a first aid station where they covered the burnt area with impregnated gauze, as a temporary measure. More than a third of his body had been burnt and he was certain to die. He was moved into the ward, and I was put to 'special' him, which only meant do my best to make his last hours as bearable as possible. His wife came, in plaster, from the women's ward to say her goodbyes, and he was heavily sedated. I came on duty the next morning, expecting to hear that he had died in the night, but he was still alive. He just hung on to life, and the moment came when the gauze would have to be removed, and the burn treated.

I went with him to the operating theatre, and once the dressing was cut off, it was appalling to see how much damage the fire had inflicted, He would certainly never walk again, but by the time I left the hospital, he was being lowered in and out of saline baths to help to speed his recovery. He faced the terrible pain with tremendous courage, and thought that he was so lucky just to be alive. I was less sure. I hated what the war did to ordinary people, who were just getting on with their lives and doing their best to cope with the horror around them. Certainly Churchill's speeches really helped to keep morale high. The 'We will never surrender' speech after Dunkirk, gave us all a sense of determination to see things through, whatever the sacrifices, and there was a common purpose that we all subscribed to. It is a pity that it needed a war to bring out the best in the British.

Even quite badly injured patients could sometimes see the black humour of the situations that faced them. I was giving a middle aged man a blanket bath, and had just reached the point, where, to preserve his dignity, I would hand him the flannel to do the very last bit himself. I stood there, by the bed, the flannel in my hands, and suddenly realised that, when he was hit by a shell, he had lost both his arms. I looked at him and he raised his eyebrows and we both smiled for we knew what came next. I was determined to hide my embarrassment, so I lifted the covering towel and, very briskly got to work with the flannel. He nearly shot out of the bed, with a cry of, "Oh. Nurse! Take it easy!", and we both laughed.

I very soon got used to being a nurse, and it was difficult to remember what it had been like in peacetime, working in an office. Fortunately, I was naturally energetic, and didn't easily get tired, and my childhood, with Buddy, had prepared me for the ups and downs of living in an institution, surrounded by other women. We were all too busy to worry that our social lives were virtually non-existent.

The air raids had filled the wards with people of all ages, and the younger men enjoyed flirting with the nurses. It was perceived as the manly thing to do. The 'ministering angel' scenario made us all very desirable, and just occasionally there would be a flicker of romance between patient and nurse. Of course, I was engaged to Ernest, but I can honestly say that I never once fancied anyone I nursed. They were patients and that was that. Thanks to the Engineers' office, I knew how to play the flirting game, which cheered everybody up, but when the over-amorous ones got discharged, I breathed a sigh of relief.

Night duty was a revelation. A Night Sister patrolled the corridors, looking in to see that everything was all right, as untrained VADs were responsible for looking after the wards. We came on duty at eight o'clock, and it would take a little time for everyone to settle down after the day staff left. The calls for one more drink, or a last bedpan, finally stopped, and the busy ward was hushed. The lights dimmed, and, apart from the odd grunt or snore, silence reigned.

It was another world. There would be jobs to do, like preparing cotton wool swabs, or rolling bandages, but, in the main, your time was your own, and it went VERY slowly! Three o'clock in the morning is, supposedly, the moment when one's life force is at its lowest ebb, and it felt like that. The wards were always warm, and there was no-one to talk to, so for me, the hardest task of all was just staying awake.

When a spell of night duty started, there seemed to be a lot of free time. One day, you came off duty at 8pm, and had twenty-four hours off, ready for when you joined the night staff the following evening. You were supposed to try to get several hours rest during the day, but, of course, you had gone to bed the previous night, so you didn't feel tired. Even if you did try to grab a nap, there were too many tempting sounds going on around you, to make any real sleep possible. What about lunch? You were hungry but your eating times would now be turned upside-down, and your main meal would come in the middle of the next night. Some people liked the comparative freedom from supervision, and the feeling of being in charge. I certainly did not.

It was lonely, and I had to stop myself waking up one of the patients for a midnight chat. I had never stayed in bed for long enough during the previous day so, not surprisingly, at about two in the morning it was a terrible struggle just to keep my eyes open. I needed the proverbial matchsticks, and dared not sit down, in case I fell asleep, so a good relaxing read was out of the question. I tidied everything in sight, inspected the patients every two minutes to see if they were awake and needed anything, and I said poems and lines from Shakespeare's plays to myself, to stop my mind filling with the total desire to lie down and close my eyes.

We were allowed to wake the patients at six o'clock, to give us time to get everyone washed and given their breakfasts, before the day staff came on at eight. I would clock-watch from about half-past four, waiting for the magic moment when I could turn the ward lights on, and rouse the sleepers. There were usually grumbles at the earliness of the hour, but I didn't mind, and a cheerful jollying-on usually carried the day.

It was on night duty in September,1940, when what looked like a spectacular sunset, appeared on the horizon. The sky blazed with golden light. I learnt the next morning that the East End, just a few miles away, had been bombed. There had been massive destruction of buildings, and a huge number of civilian casualties. I had been watching London burning.

Chapter 6

The progress of the actual war had little real impact on us at Twickenham. We were wrapped up in the task of looking after air raid casualties and the other patients. I learnt a huge amount from the trained staff I worked under. They were compassionate but very professional, and never allowed their personal feelings to affect their judgement. I got used to helping Sister lay out patients, and found death not too difficult to deal with. When I was about fourteen, Buddy had taken me to see a woman who had died at St Benedict's Nursing Home in Clapham. Ethel had been a sufferer from a particularly vicious muscular disease that contorted her features into a grotesque mask. In death the muscles relaxed and she was revealed, for the first time, as the beauty she really was. It was a lesson I never forgot.

1941 brought an exciting turn of events. I was finally called up by the army, to report to The Queen Alexandra Military Hospital in Watford, where I would, at last, be nursing soldiers. Goodbyes were said in Twickenham and with my travel warrant, (first class, of course), clutched in my little hot hand, I took the train into London and then on out to Watford, in Hertfordshire. The QA hospital was in the old orphanage, having been moved from The Embankment, in London, when the bombing started. It was a bleak red brick Victorian monstrosity, unrelieved by any of the gentler features of some nineteenth century buildings. When the doors first closed on the original inmates, they knew for sure that they were orphans, and alone in the world. I took a taxi from the station, and I was nervous, not about the nursing duties, but I had no idea how different it might be to be a Mobile VAD, in the army! In fact it was great fun.

The QA hospital was a totally different ball game from my time in the Civil Nursing Reserve at Twickenham. To start with, instead of about four VADs, there were over sixty of us, and there was a Red Cross Commandant, Lady Margaret Illingworth, who was our very own Commanding Officer. The hospital was only for men; any ATS women patients were cared for in a special out-station at Mill Hill, and each huge ward had over forty beds, filling the old orphanage dormitories. There would be about four VADs on day-duty in a ward at any one time, so we had plenty of good company for the odd chat. It was much more fun cleaning bedpans when you could laugh at the 'officer status' label. In fact, nearly everyone was from good private schools and well-off families, often with a title, or at least 'The honourable Miss...', and if you decided to transfer to the ATS, you were given an automatic commission in the army.

We slept in big dormitories, in curtained cubicles, and shared washrooms and lavatories, just like any girls' boarding school. In fact, it was very like being back at school, with Lady Margaret as our headmistress. The ward sisters were all state registered nurses, some of whom had made a pre-war career in the army. The others were often recently qualified, and were delighted to have been made ward sisters, so early in their time as trained nurses. Usually, in civilian life, they would have had to progress through being staff nurses, and the quick promotion sometimes made them guard their new status a little too keenly.

The ages of the other VADs varied from twenty-year-olds, like me, to a few fifty-year olds, mostly spinsters or widows, many of whom had been in the Red Cross for years. We came from all parts of the British Isles, though there were quite a few from the south-east of England, some of whom already knew each other socially, as they had gone to the same schools, and been debutantes together, or met at pony clubs when they were little. We all got on very well together, which was a good thing as we had virtually no privacy in the chilly rooms of the old orphanage.

The one big snag was that, as there were no ward-maids, we had to do a lot of the actual cleaning. There were a few ward orderlies, from the Royal Army Medical Corps, who helped with the nursing duties and did some of the other chores, but we were expected to turn our hands to a wide variety of non-medical jobs. One of these was cleaning the wooden floors, which had to be kept shining bright, and needed gallons of polish and lots of elbow grease. We learnt to use the 'bumpers', which were hinged on sturdy poles, with polishing cloths under flat metal plates It was a real art, swinging them from side to side, till they almost got their own rhythm, and just needed guiding. I loved the smell of the polish, and I was good at the actual 'bumping', so it became, "Dougie'll do it!", and I often got the job.

When I first arrived at Watford, I had been interviewed by Lady Margaret, our Commandant, and I realised that this was no ordinary hospital. Once the army were involved everything was affected, and we were always looking over our shoulders, to see if what we were doing was in line with 'the correct procedure'.

The very good side of life in the army hospital, was the camaraderie that existed between the VADs. Some of them stayed as friends for years after the war ended, and, in fact, Toffee was still a close friend after over fifty years. We were, rather like a boys' school, known by our surnames. 'Toffee' was Nurse Sharp, as the advertisement at the time proclaimed, "SHARP'S THE WORD FOR TOFFEE!" Of course, I was 'Dougie', as I had been all my school life, and nobody got called by their Christian name, except for some reason Eve Dunn, who was one of my very best chums. I suppose 'Dunny' was so totally unsuitable for her that, by common consent, she was always just 'Eve-Dunn', as if it was one word We laughed so much together that I find myself smiling when I write her name.

Eve came from Nottingham, where her father was a hatter, and they were very comfortably off. When she left school, she had gone into the Inland Revenue Department, and quickly became a tax officer, which I gathered was a very good job. By the time we met in the VAD, she was nearly thirty, and engaged to be married. Her fiancé was a captain in the army, and, as his surname was Walker, he was always known as 'Johnny'. Eve was getting her trousseau together, and was slightly surprised that I hadn't started to collect things for my bottom drawer. I hadn't even thought about it, but I was only just twenty, and getting married seemed a distant dream.

She was nice-looking, rather than pretty, with fair hair and blue eyes, and she had a good figure, except for her legs. They were, not to put too fine a point on it, fat. You might have said 'muscular', but certainly distinctly chunky. She wore very smart grey silky stockings and expensive shiny shoes, but nothing altered the fact that she did not have good legs, and she knew it. Fortunately she had a great sense of humour, and would be the first to joke about the disadvantages they brought, when she was making an effort to look glamorous.

Eve had always enjoyed speaking poetry aloud. She had taken the Guildhall School speech exams to improve her diction, and she had acquired a special poetry 'voice'. Her favourite poem was 'Laska' and the line, 'Laska used to ride on a mouse-grey mustang', sounded like 'Larskar yoost too ride on a maos-grey moostarng', and was guaranteed to send me into hysterics, which greatly amused her. We were on a ward together when I first went to Watford, and she was great to work with, cheerful and efficient, and good with the patients, especially those who were thoroughly depressed at being hospitalised, when there was a war going on outside. I was sure she would make Johnny Walker a very good wife.

And then he dumped her! They had been engaged for quite a long time, and it was a very nasty shock. Eve got a letter from wherever he was stationed, saying he was sorry, he had met someone else, but she could keep the engagement ring. I thought she took the news wonderfully well. She had the "There are as many good fish in the sea as ever came out of it" attitude, though she must have been terribly hurt, and I only heard the rest of the story three years later.

With Johnny out of the picture, she had almost immediately got involved with a Belgian officer she had met on leave, so it looked as though there would be a use for her trousseau after all. He proposed and Eve accepted. Then he disappeared! He had hinted that he was involved in some secret service work with the resistance movement on the continent, so she was very worried that something awful had happened. She made urgent enquiries at the Belgian Consulate in London, explaining that she was his fiancée. They broke the news to her quite gently. He was fine, but as he already had a wife in Belgium, marriage was not a possibility, at least until after the war. He had obviously run for cover when things got serious.

Nothing daunted, she found yet another suitor, this one in the Navy, and, supposedly, commander of a midget submarine. He said that his father was a laird in Scotland, and they would be married over the ship's bell. It was all very romantic. However, memories of past disappointments had made Eve cautious. On leave from the ATS, (by this time she had left the VAD and had taken a commission in the army), she travelled up to Scotland by train, and went to his village to check that everything he had said was true. Unfortunately, it wasn't. His mother was the local seamstress, and there was no sign of a father, of any kind. As Eve explained years later, it was yet another deception, and, at this point, she dumped him!

The story has a happy ending. After the war, she met and married, a charming man, who was in charge of one of the main ports in the Middle East. She brought him to see us, and both Ernest and I were very taken with him. Obviously, they were going to be living abroad, and, inevitably, we lost touch, apart from exchanging Christmas cards, but I never forgot the stories of her romances.

When, in the 1960s, a bridge friend, Doreen, suggested I have a try at writing for Mills & Boon, I decided to use Eve's adventures as the basis for a novel. So many handsome men; so much disillusionment; such a happy ending. It ought to be just the thing. Janice and I talked it over and we decided to collaborate, to make our fortunes. We named the heroine, Eve, a travel company rep, whose job took her to all the best Mediterranean resorts. (Doreen had said that the publishers liked a few exotic locations, and we could go and research the places on 'expenses', tax allowable!). Our heroine met hero number one in Minorca, (he was an officer in the regular army), and the story seemed to be working quite well, until I started to write the steamy love scene that romantic fiction demanded. I just couldn't do it. I felt like a Peeping Tom, intruding into other people's private lives. I told Doreen, who had had several books published by Mills & Boon under the pen name of Sally Wentworth, about the problem and asked how she felt when she wrote a sexy love scene. She was surprised that I had found it difficult, as she rather enjoyed those moments in the story, and we both realised that I would not, after all, be making my fortune, so it was back to the drawing board.

A nurse's uniform is often very flattering to wear, and nearly all the VADs looked good in butterfly caps, blue cotton dresses and white aprons with bold red crosses. One or two wore the older style dresses, with stiff white collars and elegant long sleeves, which, when rolled up, could be covered with frilly, white elasticised cuffs. The St John's ambulance VADs all wore light grey dresses and aprons with the black and white Maltese Cross design, and in a back cross-over fixing, instead of our neat two safety pins at the front. The hospital laundry kept everything sparklingly clean, and we would very quickly have been reprimanded if we were not correctly and smartly dressed. The patients often offered to clean our ward shoes with 'spit and polish', and it was impressive to give someone a rather scuffed pair and have them returned as if they were made of patent leather!

The real beauty among us was Joy Bowdler, 'Bowdie', who had everything a girl, in her twenties, could wish for. She had softly curling brown hair, hazel eyes and, unlike Eve Dunn, very good legs! Neither fat nor thin, her classical features and pink and white skin, made us all very envious. She had a great sense of humour, was intelligent, modest and self-effacing, and, moreover, was an excellent nurse. Of course, all the patients adored her, but she was so sweet that no-one was remotely jealous of her popularity. I kept hoping, secretly, that she would turn out to have even one little fault, but she never did. It didn't seem fair!

The social life at Watford included hockey, which I had not played at school, for the simple reason that there was no hockey field at the convent. Netball courts had been a much better use of space in Tooting, where a garden for the nuns was an essential part of their enclosed life. However, because I liked team games, I volunteered to play for our VAD hockey team, and we had matches against other nearby organisations. It was good fun, though I quickly discovered that hockey balls HURT when they hit you! Compared to netball, it was a dangerous sport, but as we had some very good players, I usually had a very easy time at left back.

My great advantage was a determination not to let anyone get past me, which often meant that, as I had never had the rules explained to me, the whistle blew when I tackled someone. However they kept me in the team, so I must have done something right. (Unless, perhaps, no-one else wanted to play!) I had a bicycle at the hospital, and on my day off, I would ride over to Enfield to see Buddy. It seemed a very long way, but it didn't cost anything, and it was lovely to be at home for a few hours. The air raids continued spasmodically, and, sadly, we were all getting quite accustomed to living in a state of war.

Chapter 7

Many of the other VADs were quite a lot older than I was. One or two had worked in the theatre before the war, and in 1941, they started to plan an entertainment for the patients at Christmas. They asked if I would like to join in whatever they did, and I loved the idea. They had decided to write a pantomime, and chose 'Cinderella', which sounded great fun. We were to have a Prince Charming, (Bowdie would be perfect for the role), a lovely Cinders, (there were several pretty little blondes in our ranks), two Ugly Sisters, the King, the Fairy Godmother, and, of course, Buttons. They organised some auditions in off-duty times, and there was a very encouraging response.

Their very good script started in verse.

> *"You all must know that Pantomime,*
> *Traditionally is in rhyme,*
> *But we, I fear, have not succeeded.*
> *We found that too much brain was needed.*
> *So just to lend the proper touch,*
> *We've rhymed a bit, (but not too much!)."*

We were all terribly impressed, and I was delighted to be offered the role of Buttons, which was rather wistful comedy. The director asked if I had any special acting skills, as they needed someone to do something in front of the curtain, while they changed a set. I had always enjoyed Stanley Holloway's monologues, like 'Albert and the Lion', so I promised to see if there was one that would suit a pantomime in an army hospital.. I got the book from Watford Library, and to my delight there was 'The Battle of Hastings', which I thought the patients would enjoy.

"I'll tell of the Battle of Hastings, as happened in days long gone by, When Duke William became King of England, and Harold got shot in the eye!"

Of course I would drop all the H's, and I could do a reasonably good northern accent, which settled the 'voice' to use for Buttons. The producer immediately approved my solo act, and probably thought that, even if it wasn't entertaining, the patients wouldn't be too critical, and it would solve the scene changing problem.

We had huge fun rehearsing in our spare time, and I could see it was going to be a really good show. Lady Margaret was very proud of our efforts, which she managed to see as an affirmation of our commitment to the Red Cross, and the Colonel, who was the commanding officer of the hospital, accepted an invitation to attend. There was to be only one performance, which would take place in the main hall where, doubtless, the poor little orphans had once gathered for miserable assemblies.

As always, there were people who could do everything when the occasion demanded. We had a very good pianist for any songs, busy fingers sewed some imaginative costumes, (Bowdie had a real Prince Charming outfit with high boots and a very smart Cavalier-type hat that sported a huge feather), and the problem of the coach was solved by using a decorated theatre trolley. The Ugly Sisters were padded out with pillows from the wards, and my costume was simply blue hospital trousers and jacket, decorated with very large buttons. At the dress rehearsal, I was asked to improvise some patter, with a few jokes, to make the scene part of the Cinderella story, and I really looked forward to the actual performance the following day.

There were two sets. The kitchen at the Palace for the "You shall go to the Ball!" scene with Cinders and the Fairy Godmother, (played by the oldest VAD who had shining white hair, which gave the role an unexpected sophistication), and the Prince's Ballroom, using the hospital's Christmas decorations to full effect. Bright paper chains made by the patients and a decorated tree from one of the wards, became a festive background to the Ball. My scene before the curtain, came as they changed the décor, and I just hoped that the backstage helpers would do it a bit quicker than they had done at the dress rehearsal, when it had taken about ten minutes.

On the day of the performance, the hall was packed out by five o'clock, with the CO in the centre of the front row, flanked by Lady Margaret and her staff on one side and the hospital's doctors and senior QAs on the other. The pianist struck up 'God Save the King', and the entire audience sprang to attention, standing till the last note had died away, and the show had begun.

Everyone had a great time. The patients seemed to enjoy every minute, and joined in enthusiastically when we divided the audience into two parts and did the 'Pack Up Your Troubles' and 'It's a Long Way to Tipperary' singsong It was a traditional panto, except that there weren't any men in it, and when I did my Stanley Holloway monologue in front of the curtain, I got thunderous applause. At the end the Colonel came up on stage to thank us, (a bit like royalty at a command performance), and Lady Margaret beamed with delight. We all felt we had made Christmas in hospital a bit happier for everyone, including ourselves.

None of the patients were battle casualties. They were all in specialist units – but just being in the army didn't stop men getting ordinary things wrong with them. We had soldiers who had to have an appendix removed, men with pneumonia, contracted after long spells under canvas, wearing damp clothes, and there were the usual broken bones to be put in plaster, deep accidental cuts to be stitched, and patients with infectious diseases, like mumps and measles, to be nursed.

A very surprising case was a young corporal, who had a very bad squint. One eye was totally out of sync with the other one. The difference was so marked that it was hard to understand why he had not had an operation while he was still at school. It must have made life very difficult for him, as he had to wear very strong corrective glasses, not to mention the fact that it looked absolutely awful. I saw him when he was first admitted, and then after the operation, when he had a huge bandage over both eyes. He managed very well for the week when he was effectively blind, and I was really interested to see what difference the operation had made. I was told to take off the bandage, and get him ready for the eye specialist to check that all was well.

It was an amazing result. As I took away the final piece of gauze and gently bathed the eye, I saw an unimaginable change. He looked wonderful, and no longer cross-eyed. I gave him a hand-mirror to let him see how successful the operation had been and he could hardly believe the change. For the first time in his life, he looked really handsome, and when he was discharged to go back to his unit, I was sure that his life would be totally altered. At least the war had done somebody some good.

The QA Sisters were, on the whole, efficient and pleasant, for it was useful to have the VADs in the role that probationers would have played in a training hospital. We did all the bed-making, bottle and bedpan giving, locker tidying, and food serving, as well as most of the cleaning. Sisters would busy round the ward, with sharp eyes that spotted any omission, however small, and there was, certainly, one way in which the army hospital was quite different from the civilian one at Twickenham, and that was 'regulations'.

Not only did the sheet have to be turned down the correct length over the counterpane, but the beds had to be in a perfect line along the sides of the ward. The wooden floor planks gave markers, and every bed had its wheels turned inwards and then the metal end of the bed, placed on the line of the floor board. In the bedside lockers, the hospital blue jacket and trousers had to be folded in a certain way, and kept on the right shelf. Even toothbrushes, toothpaste and flannels had an order in which they were stored, but after a while I stopped querying the army's strange rules.

Just once, I fell out with one of the QAs, and was hauled in front of Lady Margaret to be reprimanded. I was on night duty, which meant that there were just the two of us on the ward, and we had a patient who was in a great deal of pain. At about two o'clock in the morning, I saw that he was awake, and asked him if he wanted anything. "Oh, yes please, nurse," he whispered, "I'd love a cup of tea, if it isn't too much trouble."

I promised him that I would make him one at once, and hurried off to the ward kitchen to put the kettle on.

Because tea was rationed, the ward's supply was kept in a locked cupboard, so I went to Sister's room and asked for the key, explaining which patient had asked for a drink of tea. Sister listened coldly, and said, 'No, he can't have one, there isn't much tea left and I shall need it for the medical officer when he does his rounds. Go and ask him if he would like a cup of cocoa?" I was furious, particularly as I was certain that he wouldn't. He was really disappointed, but accepted that there would be no tea forthcoming, and he certainly didn't want cocoa. He told me not to worry, it didn't matter. Ah, but it did. It mattered to me!

I knew it wasn't a wise thing to do, but I was so angry that I threw caution to the winds, and went to try to get Sister to change her mind, I pointed out that the tea ration was intended for the patients, not for the staff, and that the man, who was very ill, did not want a cup of cocoa. I was sure that, when she thought about it, she would realise that it was important that we did our best to make, what might be his last days, happy. Please could I have the key?

She tried to freeze me with a look, but I was so annoyed that I barely noticed it, and I was about to push the argument further, when in icy tones, she said, "That will be all, Nurse! ", turned on her heel and walked away into the ward. The following day I was called to Lady Margaret's office. Apparently Sister had reported me for insolence, and I was asked to explain why I had behaved so badly, and let down the entire VAD contingent. I recounted what had happened, but I could see that the system did not allow forgiveness of any breach of rank status. My punishment was to have my promotion to Grade 1, which carried extra pay, postponed for three months, and, needless to say, I was moved back to day duty on a different ward.

It was, I suppose, to my credit, that I didn't get Sister into trouble, as I could have done. She had regularly taken an unauthorised nap in her room each night, and had instructed me to wake her immediately if I heard Night Sister arriving. I had saved her bacon on several occasions, but the old school tenet of not 'telling on someone', stopped me making sure she got her just desserts.

The next time I was on night duty, it was for three days, covering for another VAD who was on brief compassionate leave. The quite small ward, in an annexe to the main building, specialised in sexually transmitted diseases, 'STD', the bane of armies from time immemorial. I knew none of the staff and it seemed a wonderful time to try out a totally different voice. Because I was 'Nurse Douglas', patients were always asking where, in Scotland, I came from. My father's family came from Fife, so I would use that as an answer. Almost always came the remark, "Then why haven't you got a Scottish accent, nurse?", and if I wasn't too busy, or I thought they needed cheering up, I would switch to my best Edinburgh voice, which they always loved. I didn't know if it was any good, never having been to Edinburgh, or anywhere else in Scotland for that matter.

When, the next evening, I reported to the Sister on the STD ward, I used my new voice, and no one seemed remotely surprised. I suppose you don't expect a twenty-one year old nurse to be putting on a funny accent. The patients, who were a jolly lot, were all English, and they quickly christened me, 'Little Nurse Jock'. They asked where I came from and I told them that my father came from Fife, which was true and satisfied their curiosity. I had a great time, though it was quite hard to remember to keep the accent up all night, with everyone.

Then, on the next evening, I was greeted with the news that there was a new patient on the ward, and they were tickled to bits. "Guess where he comes from, Nurse?" they asked. "He's from Fife. too!" At this moment the man appeared from the washroom. He was in his late twenties, and looked a little downcast. I took the bull by the horns, "I hear you're from Fife," I remarked, in my best Scottish tones. He looked at me for a moment, and I thought the game was up. "Ah, Nurrrse, "he said, "It's say guid tay he-ah the voice!". As I just said, you don't expect a grown woman to be putting on a funny accent.

The war had now been on for more than two years, and Ernest and I had managed to meet on leave several times in London. We had gone to the theatres that had been reopened after the initial close-down, or out to eat at one of the restaurants serving a fixed five shilling evening meal. He came to stay in Enfield, under Buddy's sharp eye, but the nearly three years we had been engaged, did seem a long time. There was always the chance that The Royal Devon Yeomanry would get posted to somewhere like North Africa, where there was quite a lot of action, and he suggested that we should now think seriously about getting married. I was twenty-one, so I didn't need anyone's permission, and I promised to give the idea serious thought. Maybe in the summer? If we were both still alive and kicking!

Chapter 8

The more I thought about it, the more attractive the prospect seemed, of getting married in 1942, for it felt as if the war would go on for ever. When I looked at the map of Europe and saw that Hitler's forces were apparently in control of everywhere, except Switzerland, Spain and Sweden, a quick result in our favour, looked unlikely. It was not that I thought we might lose the war, but actually winning it, did look a long way off. When I broached the idea with Buddy, she didn't raise any objections, though she wondered when and where I wanted to tie the knot. We were Catholics, and the Enfield church had been destroyed in an air raid, so services were being held in a temporary wooden hut. She thought that, perhaps, this was not exactly what I had in mind, and she was right!

The best place to be married, it seemed to me, would be Kensington, which I knew quite well, and would be central for our wedding guests to get to, by bus and train. There were some magnificent Catholic churches in London, like Farm Street, run by the Jesuits, where all the really smart people went to mass, and, of course, the Brompton Oratory, which I had visited several times. I asked my VAD friends what they thought, and they all plumped for the Oratory, mostly, I suspected, because they knew that Harrods was just round the corner. Quite how I could get married in fashionable Kensington, when I was nursing in Watford, and had a home address in Enfield, was not immediately obvious, so I gave it some serious thought. It was definitely a challenge.

At the time, all church marriages were preceded by the calling of banns. This was done for three successive weeks, at the church in the bride's parish, where the actual service would take place. It was not therefore, just a question of booking a Saturday at the Oratory for us to marry, but having an address in Kensington to use for the banns. I came up with, what I thought, was an ingenious plan. Find an advertisement for a bed-sitting room, to rent nearby, take it for a month, and use that address. A lot of property in London had been emptied by the air raid menace, and it was not difficult to get places for short term lets, in fashionable areas.

On my next day off, I went by train and tube to Kensington, and looked at all the rooms advertised in shop windows. I found a perfect one, just off the Brompton Road, a bit expensive, but within our reach, so I went round to see it at once. It was a very pleasant Victorian mansion flat, owned by a man in his sixties, who was, presumably, retired. His daughter was in the forces and he let two rooms to help to pay the bills. I explained why I would only need the room for a month, possibly in July or August, and that I would not be staying there, because I was a VAD. He looked a bit disappointed by the shortness of the let, but cheered up when I paid the month's rent in advance. I took a careful note of the address, and made my way round to the Oratory to ask about possible dates.

I met a charming priest who was tremendously helpful, and looked at the days Ernest and I had agreed to try for. It would be on a Saturday in August, and the 15th was our number one choice. By sheer chance, he said, there was a slot free for 2.30pm on that day, as long as I wouldn't mind the church being already decorated with masses of flowers, as it was the feast of the Assumption. It would be impossible to change the floral arrangements, if I wanted to have a special effect. This was a great load off my mind as I was pretty sure that the florists in Kensington, like Constance Spry, were all very expensive. I immediately asked for a firm booking for Saturday, August 15th, 1942. There were minor points to settle like the fee for the organist, the music we wanted and whether or not to have the red carpet on the Oratory steps, but such things could all wait till I had told Ernest the good news

What should I wear? I would need lots of clothing coupons for my trousseau, for, unlike Eve Dunn, I hadn't thought ahead. For a wedding dress, someone suggested getting one made from curtain fabric that I could buy from Liberty's without coupons. Trying not to imagine what a fright I might look prancing down the aisle in chintz, I went to see what was on offer, and they were absolutely right. There was one material, in cream and gold damask, which could be made into a wonderful gown, and Buddy knew a very good dressmaker in Enfield. Problem solved.

There was so much to do on my days off, and such a lot to talk through with Ernest when he got leave, that it seemed we would never get everything done. Uncle Frank agreed to give me away, Buddy sent out invitations to the hundred or so people we wanted to come to the wedding, and booked a reception buffet at the Rembrandt Hotel in the Brompton Road. Ernest ordered top hat and formal suit from Moss Bros, and asked his school chum, Ronnie, who was a sub-lieutenant in the navy, to be best man. My special friend from the convent, Evelyn, who was in the Foreign Office, was delighted to be the bridesmaid, and even bought her own dress, with her own clothing coupons. Who could have asked for more? We chose a week's honeymoon at a farm in the Quantock Hills in Somerset, and kept our fingers crossed that there would be no sudden escalation of the war before September.

When I look at the wedding photos, it all comes back! The golden birds I had, unaccountably, chosen as a headdress, and Ernest holding his top hat, because it was so much too big that it slipped down over his eyes. Ronnie and Evelyn, both looking slightly stressed, and the VADs, en masse, having great fun. Buddy and I had come, from Enfield, to Kensington in a limousine, and we had started much too soon. One of Buddy's biggest hang-ups was timing. She was always much too early for any meeting, and when I would arrive at the agreed time, she had usually been waiting for at least half an hour. This had the unfortunate effect of making me feel I was late, so I often got to any rendezvous half an hour early, so that I could be there first. Once she realised what I was doing, she would arrive even earlier, so it was a no-win situation!

Our wedding car got to Hyde Park before two o'clock, and so we had to drive around to kill time. People, sitting on the grass, enjoying a lovely summer's day, looked up and, seeing a bride, gave cheerful waves. By the time we had done two more circuits, they weren't even bothering to look. I could almost hear them saying, "Oh, it's only that bride again!" We got to the Oratory just in time for me to take Uncle Frank's arm and start down the very long aisle to the tune of the Wedding March. The huge church looked almost empty; a hundred people only filled the first few rows, so I whispered that maybe we should move a bit faster, and we positively scurried till we reached the first row of guests.

The service went without a hitch, though I kept feeling as though I was an onlooker, rather than part of the action, and found myself listening to the seriousness of phrases like, 'forsaking all others, and thereto I plight thee my troth'. However, we both said 'I do', quite confidently and very soon had signed the marriage register, and been photographed in front of the church. (The steps were covered in red carpet, as they hadn't had time to take it up after the previous wedding!) We crossed the road to the reception and were enthusiastically kissed and congratulated. There was a wonderfully funny moment when the wedding cake was wheeled in, apparently covered in glistening white icing. Before it could be cut, the 'icing' was lifted off, as it was made of decorated cardboard. The rationing of sugar had made real icing a non-starter.

By the time we had changed into our going-away outfits, (in my case a dark green jacket and a brown checked skirt), had got to Waterloo, and caught the train, we were both very tired, and it was quite late before we finally arrived in Somerset, and took a taxi from Barnstaple to the farm. It was all we'd hoped for, tucked away in lush woodland, and after a welcoming cup of tea, we headed for bed. Hardly surprisingly, we both fell fast asleep as soon as our heads touched the very comfortable pillows. The meaningful looks we got from the farmer's wife when she brought us our breakfast in bed and said, in a broad Somerset accent, "Oi 'ope yews slep' wol !", seemed very funny. If she had only known, we actually had.

Of course, we had a wonderful honeymoon. The weather was warm and sunny, and we were young and in love. For a few days we forgot that there was a war on, so we enjoyed each other's company, and ate the most wonderful farm food. I had forgotten the delicious taste of thick cream and freshly churned butter, and the eggs were often less than a day old when we ate them. 'Kilton Farm' had its own flock of sheep, and a special joint of roast lamb one day was like Sunday dinners before the days of rationing.

We went on buses to the coast, about three miles away, and I persuaded Ernest to try riding at the local stable, even though he was not at all keen on the idea. It nearly ended in disaster. They let us ride in a five acre field behind the stables, and half way round, Ernest's horse suddenly decided it was time to go back home. It turned and took off at speed, down the middle of the field, with my new husband clinging on for dear life. To my horror, I could see a five barred gate at the bottom of the field, apparently right across their path, and I realised that Ernest would be thrown as the horse jumped it. There was nothing I could do, though what I could not see was a wide gap in the hedge, next to the gate, which the horse went through quite safely, and came to a halt in the stable yard. The shaken rider was loudly protesting that he would NEVER get on a horse again, and, as far as I know, he never did.

It was a really sad moment when we both had to get back into uniform, and return to our duties as soldier and nurse. It would be three months before we could spend another week's leave together, and that seemed like ages away. Fortunately, Ernest had been given an opportunity to transfer to the Intelligence Corps, and I had just been moved from Watford, to the Guards' Depot at Caterham, so we both had new challenges to keep us busy.

Caterham turned out to be very different from the hospital in Watford. It was an out station, and there was a QA in charge, but most of the patients had only 'minor ailments', so there were no real medical facilities. Rather like a cottage hospital, cuts could be stitched and wounds dressed, but anything major was transferred elsewhere. A young army doctor was on call, and did the occasional ward round, but the nurses virtually ran the show. Strangely, I have completely forgotten my colleagues at the Caterham Barracks, perhaps because there was no feeling of solidarity, as there had been at Watford. However, I do remember the patients very clearly, as they were all guardsmen, up to their eyes in the army's ethos, and subscribing to it, lock, stock and barrel.

It was fascinating to watch army spit and polish in action. Once any immediate medical problem had disappeared, to my amazement, totally off their own bat, the boots were out and the whole process began. It was real spit that they mixed with the polish, and the effect was quite dramatic. I had never thought to see my face reflected in the toe of an army boot, but I almost could.

The peaked caps, obligatory in the Guards, really looked uncomfortable. They were worn so far forward that the narrow peak obscured their view of the immediate surroundings. Then they got me to try one on, and I couldn't see anything unless I bent my neck so far backwards, that it actually hurt.. They hooted with laughter at my complaints and explained that that was exactly the point. You had to walk with your head tilted back which they felt made guardsmen look very smart. They took a lot of photos, of groups, standing in self-conscious lines. "You stand in the middle, Nurse, and it'll make my wife jealous!" It was all harmless fun, like the Engineers' Department at Scotland Yard.

We were made very conscious of drill going on nearby, by the hammer of stamping boots on tarmac that went on all day with the voices of the drill sergeants echoing through the air, like frustrated caged predators at the zoo. The patients often watched the parade ground through the ward windows, and made jokes about the ineptitude of the current platoons of new recruits, and the muffled swear words that were being directed at them. They persuaded me to learn how to do rifle drill with the ward broom, and beamed with satisfaction when I could "Present arms! Port arms! Slope arms!" without making a mistake. It cheered them up, and that seemed to me to be very important, in view of the likely fate of many guardsmen, when the final battle for Europe was joined.

The three month gap between one leave and the next, went by surprisingly quickly, and, in November, Ernest and I had our first week as a married couple in Enfield, in our own bed, in our own room. We spent the time doing ordinary things and trying to believe that the war would soon be over. Ernest liked the training for the Intelligence Corps, including learning some Japanese, which was a bit worrying, and he loved my tales of life with the Guards at Caterham. Our future was terribly uncertain, and didn't bear thinking about, but we couldn't resist making plans for the peace that must finally come. We talked about buying our very own house, and we both liked the idea of Surrey, but we did not discuss the number of children we might have, it would have seemed like tempting fate. The unspoken agreement was that we would wait till the war was over, and see how things turned out.

Things certainly did not turn out quite as we expected, for about six weeks later, I found that I was pregnant. If all went well, the doctor told me, the baby would arrive at the end of August, which certainly did not fit in with our plans. Ernest accepted the news philosophically. I don't think he could quite take in the fact that he was going to be a father, with all that that entailed, for no-one knew where they would be the following August. My immediate response was to do all I could to try to get a miscarriage. I ran everywhere, went for long cycle rides, and took very hot baths galore. The only result was that I had never been fitter, or cleaner, in my entire life.

Of course, by the time that three months had gone by, and I had accepted the fait accompli, I had to warn the army authorities that I would be leaving the service to become a housewife. Naturally, being the army, there was a set procedure to be gone through, to effect my honourable discharge, and the wheels were set in motion. It emerged that I could continue till the end of May, but that they would transfer me, with immediate effect, to the out-station where members of the ATS were nursed. It was to be, "Goodbye, Caterham", and "Hello, Mill Hill!"

The new posting had some advantages. Mill Hill was much nearer Enfield for my visits to see Buddy, and the wards were not next to an army barracks. When I got there to report for duty, I could see that it looked like a large detached private house, with a nice garden in, what the estate agents call, 'a good location'. As I went in through the open front door, and into the hall, all I could see were someone's legs at the top of a pair of steps. I nearly gasped, for I knew those legs! Unless I was mistaken, the rest of the body would turn out to be Eve Dunn, and, of course, it was. She was the VAD in charge of the ATS out-station, and was absolutely delighted that we were going to work together again. I had, temporarily, lost touch with her when I was posted to Caterham, and she had only just been told that "Mobile VAD Grade One / Douglas, J.E.", was about to join her staff.

Eve showed me around, and there seemed to be only two wards, with one or two smaller rooms on the first floor. Apparently, many of the patients were not ill but merely pregnant, and, as almost all of them were unmarried, they had found difficulty in deciding what to do about the baby. The alternatives were quite simple. Keep the baby, which meant leaving the service, or try for an adoption. Some of women were actually in denial, and insisted that they weren't pregnant at all. There must be something else wrong, that gave identical symptoms. One patient even protested that it just wasn't possible for her to be expecting a baby, as she didn't know any men. She could only suppose, she said, that when she had taken a nap on a park bench one evening, she must have been molested in her sleep.

My bedroom was on the second floor and very comfortable and Eve's was next to it, but rather bigger as she was 'in charge'. There was no night duty, as none of the patients were ill, and after everyone had gone to bed, I knocked on Eve's door, to have a chat about the latest VAD gossip. I was really surprised when I was finally invited to "Come in!", that Eve was wearing a visible plug in either ear. She told me that, as a very light sleeper, she was constantly disturbed in the early hours, by donkeys calling to each other over the fields at the back of the house. Hence the ear plugs. Her love life was, for the moment, going well and she seemed relaxed and happy. I was sure that we would have fun working together, and it was an ideal way to end to my career in His Majesty's Service.

Chapter 9

By 1942, the war had entered a new phase. The Japanese attack on Pearl Harbour, in December, 1941, was followed by a quick expansion of violence across Asia. The impossible happened when the impregnable base of Singapore fell in February, to a surprise land invasion. All the guns had been trained on to the approaches by sea. India was threatened and Malaysia and Burma came under attack. By the end of the year, the situation in Asia looked very dangerous. In China, the Nationalist leader, Chiang Kai Shek and the Communist forces under Mao Tse Tung kept the resistance alive, but their political differences were so great that they were in no sense, allies. The entry of the United States into the war, on our side, cheered everyone up, and though rationing was tight, we all felt that the huge resources of North America meant we couldn't be starved out by the enemy's U boats. The Russians were beginning to overcome the German invasion, but it was a desperately slow process in a huge country.

When the end of May came, I said au revoir to Eve Dunn, adieu to Mill Hill, and went to join Buddy in Enfield. She was delighted at the thought of having a grandchild and, because she couldn't knit, she crocheted little matinee coats, bootees, bonnets and mittens, ready for the new arrival. Pink or blue? It seemed safer to have white or yellow, but I was convinced that the baby would be a boy, and I didn't even think of a name for a girl. My choice for a boy was 'Paul'. It went well with Norris, and wasn't easily lengthened or abbreviated. Robert, my father's name would be there too, and Ernest had a family name, Winn, always given to the eldest son. 'Paul Robert Winn Norris' certainly sounded very good.

Shopping for things for the new baby, was great fun. Dear little Vyella vests and nighties, jackets, leggings and bobble hats for the coming winter. Lots of nappies, all needing clothing coupons, a baby bath tub, and, of course, a pram. Buddy was adamant, that it had to be one of the big, coach-sprung variety that nannies wheeled around Kensington Gardens and we managed to get a second hand maroon one, in brand new condition, totally scratch free.. It was certainly impressive but the real piece de resistance was the cot. Buddy had a patient on the district, whose daughter decorated cots. We ordered a crib, a dream in blue and white muslin, all frills and bows, and it now stood in my bedroom, waiting for that baby.

There were still two months to go, so Buddy suggested that we take the train down to Cornwall, to get some sea air and see the West Country. She booked us in to a farm, just outside Perranporth, on the north Cornish coast, and asked them to hire two bikes for us, so that we could explore the area. We were on half board and hoped we would have a chance to try the world famous. 'Cornish Pasties'. We needn't have worried, because we had them for supper on our arrival.

"Ah, Cornish pasties!" we cried excitedly, "How delicious!" They were, certainly, very filling. We wondered what we would have for supper the next day. Perhaps fish, as the farm was only a couple of miles from the coast? But, no, we had Cornish pasties again. "Ah, Cornish pasties!" we said. "That's nice. Maybe tomorrow we'll have fish? Or the local crab?" But we didn't, and by the end of the week, neither of us ever wanted to see another Cornish pasty again But, of course it was war-time, so there was some excuse and, fortunately, the breakfasts were wonderful, so all was forgiven.

We had great fun cycling along the narrow lanes, and caused quite a stir when we met people out walking. I was seven and a half moths pregnant, and by that time it can no longer remain a secret, even in a smock! "Look at that girl," they would say in loud voices, "she's pregnant! Fancy riding a bike when you're pregnant!" I caused an even greater furore on the beach at Perranporth, when I hired a board to try the fun of surfing. I'd had to cut my swimsuit into two pieces to accommodate the bulge, but it was perfectly decent. When I walked across the beach to the sea, carrying the surf board, it was very clear what I was going to do. "Look at that girl," they cried with horror, "she's going to go surfing! She'll never do it!...." As it happened they were probably right, as it was impossible to lie flat on your stomach, when you're seven months pregnant, and I fell off the surf board, every time I tried.

Our Cornish farm had a litter of wire-haired terrier-cross puppies, and wanted good homes for them. They were irresistible, so we chose one to take back to Enfield, on the train. We named him 'Perry', after the scene of my surfing fiasco, and he was one of the cleverest dogs I have ever owned. In a very short time, he could do the most amazing 'tricks' to order. He could beg, die for the district nurses, shut the door, play the piano, speak, shake hands, give a kiss, and so on. Visitors could be entertained by any, or all, of these wonderful accomplishments, though "Shut the door!" rather backfired, for, often, when you had just opened the door to carry a tea-tray into the kitchen, Perry would shut it before you could get through!

Unfortunately, I had not taught him the most important lesson of all; obedience. He would run off into the road the minute the front door was opened, and would disappear around the corner. When he was brought back, or we collected him from the police station, we would hear stories of the accidents he had very nearly caused. I did everything I could to try to train him to "Stay!", but to no avail. He was a farm dog at heart, and wanted the freedom to run in the fields, so, reluctantly, we gave him to a farm on the outskirts of town, and replaced him with a much less volatile pedigree Scottie, we named 'Andy'.

Back from Cornwall, it was now very close to the end of my pregnancy and I was booked into The Royal Northern Hospital on the Holloway Road, as a paying patient. Buddy had insisted that I should go to a 'voluntary' hospital, rather than to Chase Farm, which was much nearer. We had everything ready, and I was keen to 'get the agony over', so when I felt the first pain on the afternoon of August 27th, it was all systems go.

I shall not go into the traumas of childbirth,, except to say that, because I hadn't been to pre-natal classes, when the midwife said,

"PUSH!", I thought she meant me to push her. She had my feet on her chest at the time, so I gave a good shove and sent her sprawling across the delivery room, knocking over the instrument trolley as she staggered backwards. She was not amused, but a beautiful baby boy, weighing nearly nine pounds, was duly delivered by the stork. Buddy heard the good news when she rang the hospital first thing in the morning, and we still have the telegram she sent to Ernest in Northern Ireland:

"Paul arrived safely at 3.30 am. Mother and baby both doing well."

Ten days later, a taxi took me home and, at last, the pretty little blue and white cot in my room, had a bonny little blue-eyed occupant.

It is surprising how quickly one gets into a routine with a baby. There wasn't a spare moment for anything else, as breast feeding was very time consuming. Bottles could be held by anyone, but nursing mothers had to sit, switching from one side to the other and the process took ages. However, it was good for the baby, saved money, and I didn't have any problems, so I persevered. Feeding time for the lions at the zoo was only once a day, but babies had a four hourly schedule from 6 am to 10 pm. In between, they had to be changed and bathed, clothes and nappies had to be washed, meals prepared and the daily routine of family life continued. I just couldn't see how anyone could deal with more than one child. Interestingly, Buddy's neighbour had twin boys and remarked that she wouldn't wish twins on her worst enemy. I was lucky, as I lived with my mother, a nurse, had no other children, and we had domestic help for the housework. How on earth did less fortunate mothers manage?.

On my second day home I proudly put the baby in the pram, and took the short trip down into the town to do some shopping. I walked slowly and carefully, to Sainsbury's, in the High Street. It was a bright sunny day, and the world seemed a good place to live in, with my new baby. Buddy had given me a shopping list, so I put the pram outside the shop, making sure that the brake was on, and went into the store. There were several things to buy, and queuing at the counter waiting to be served, I remembered one or two other things we needed. The assistant finally served me and I walked home, wondering if there had been anything else I should have bought.

Buddy was waiting for me when I got in, and we unpacked the shopping bag together. I said I hoped I'd got everything, as I had a feeling that there was something I'd forgotten. She asked me how the baby had been, and I let out a gasp. That was it!. He must still be in the pram, outside Sainsbury's. Buddy cried, "You wicked girl! How could you forget your baby?" She jumped on her bicycle and went, like the wind, off to the shop. I followed on foot, and was relieved to find that all was well. He hadn't been stolen, but it was a measure of what a very new mother I was.

Ernest arrived the next day, having been given a brief compassionate leave to meet his little son. He was delighted to see such a healthy-looking baby boy, with fair hair and blue eyes, like the rest of his family, and laughed when Buddy told him about the Sainsbury's adventure. His other news was rather worrying, as they had been warned that six of his unit in the Intelligence Corps were to be attached to the West African Brigade and that he was one of the group. They had had instruction in some Japanese phrases, and, if any prisoners were taken, he could ask "What is your name, and what is your number?" He tried the questions out on me and I didn't point out that they would have a rather limited use, as he certainly wouldn't understand the reply.

Ernest told us that the most likely scenario was that they would go by sea to Lagos, get to know the Africans they would be working with, and then go on, with them, to India. From there they would travel to Burma, where the battle had already been joined. He would be away for some time. The good news, as far as I was concerned, was that he would not be involved in any attack on Hitler's armies on the continent, where I was sure there would be a huge number of casualties. He would be a long way away, but I felt that he might be a little safer in Burma, and he would get a week's leave before they embarked for Nigeria.

In November, Ernest and I had a final week together in Enfield, before he left for West Africa. The baby was almost three months old, and though we didn't know it at the time, he would be three, before he saw his father again. Such was the disruption that came with war. Blissfully ignorant of the long parting to come, we had a super week. Leaving Buddy baby-sitting, when we went up to London to see a wonderfully satirical revue at the Ambassadors Theatre. It was called 'Sweet and Low' and starred Hermione Gingold, who did an unforgettable number called 'The Grasshopper's Dance' that was side-splittingly funny. We did all the ordinary things that had become so extraordinary since 1939, like walking in the park, and doing the shopping. Ernest went to say goodbye to his family in Crofton Park and I promised that, as soon as possible, I would take the baby there, to see his other grandmother.

Paul was a very good baby, and, by now, had his own nursery, so that I could get a good night's sleep. Buddy's room also overlooked the garden, and she was a very light sleeper, so quite often, if Paul woke in the night, she would be up and dealing with whatever was wrong, before I had properly woken up. Buddy was very anxious that we should have a good regime for the baby, which did not allow any bad habits, so Paul was never given a dummy to keep him quiet. There was, however, a wonderfully useful liquid called 'Gripewater', a spoonful of which would usually send him back to sleep. I didn't ask what it contained, but I suspected that there was some medicinal ingredient that did the trick, as there was a warning on the bottle about 'too frequent use'!

1943 did bring some very good news. After several false alarms, Peggy's husband, Dick, was repatriated from his German prison camp. He had been injured after Dunkirk, and, unfortunately, his damaged spine had worsened, and he was brought home, as a non-combatant, in a spinal carriage. She was, of course, overjoyed, as he had been away for three long years. I was delighted, as I had always liked Dick, and his father, Ted, and had got very friendly with Hugh, one of his cousins, who lived not too far away. Peggy was very keen to start a family, so they decided to adopt a new-born baby girl, whom they named Teresa.

Ernest wrote as regularly as possible, and we heard all about Nigeria. His letters were tremendously interesting and full of fascinating details about the West African Brigade. He sent us a packet of dried banana slices, which were delicious, and told me to expect a pair of heads in ebony, that he had watched being made in Lagos. They were beautifully carved and still sit on our mantelpiece to this day, over sixty years later. As far as we could tell, there were no immediate plans for the next stage of the journey, which would take them to the north of India, but he was definitely seeing the world. We showed Paul his picture every day, and we said "Good night, Daddy!" to the photo every bedtime, but it was a poor substitute for the real thing.

Chapter 10

By the summer of 1944, I was getting restless. So many friends were working, or in the forces, and I felt terribly lazy, staying at home all day. The baby was nearly a year old, and, in Enfield, there were excellent day nurseries that working mothers could use. I had joined 'The Film Artistes Association' in the hope of earning a little money as a film extra, and was very excited to be called to the West End, for a casting session for the film 'Caesar and Cleopatra'. Of course, I fantasised about getting 'discovered', and the scenario included meeting an admiring casting director, who immediately spotted my innate ability. Failing that, I would settle for an extremely well-paid minor role.

The session was held in a particularly dreary hall, in a back street off Piccadilly, and when I got there, the rows of benches were full of hopeful, would-be film extras, of every age, colour and size. There were still some spaces at the back of the hall, so I squeezed past the end of the benches, until I found somewhere to sit. I couldn't think how the actual casting process was going to work. How on earth could they sort out who they wanted, from the two hundred or so men, women and children who had turned up, and were sitting in rows, like patients in a doctor's surgery? I soon got my answer.

There was a table and three chairs at the front of the hall, and almost immediately after I arrived, three people came in and sat down. The man in the centre gave a very short instruction on what we were to do, which turned out to be, stand up one row at a time, so that he could decide who would be engaged, and then sit down quietly, while the next row was inspected. Not quite the audition I had expected! His face looked faintly familiar, but I couldn't think why, and the process quickly started. The first row were asked to stand, and he pointed at several people, saying, "You...you...and...you", and that was it. "Next row, please," and his performance was repeated. It was like choosing tins off a shelf, without any finesse whatsoever. I looked at the faces of the ones who hadn't been 'chosen', and they were totally disconsolate. I decided not to risk the humiliation of joining their ranks, so when my row was told to stand, I remained seated, and, of course, unselected.

On the way out, as we filed slowly past the table where the chosen ones were giving their names and addresses to the other two officials, I remembered with awful clarity why I recognised him. At Twickenham, in 1940, I had nursed him. In fact I had been put on to 'special' him in a private room. He was suffering, at the time, from a nasty bout of syphilis, and we had spent a lot of time in each other's company. Would he recognise me? I was just walking past him when, suddenly, he looked up and our eyes met.

It must have been an uncomfortable moment for him, but he smiled brightly and said, "Nurse Douglas! What are you doing here?" I muttered something about the film, and he asked if I had been selected to be an extra. When I shook my head, he turned to his assistant and said "Take her name!" and to me, "It was nice to see you again!", and promptly disappeared out of the hall. They did, in fact, send me an invitation to join the cast, but I would have had to report to Elstree, for make-up at about 5.30 am every morning, and it was a very long cycle ride from Enfield. Somehow the vibes weren't quite right, so I politely declined the offer and my career in films never got started.

Meantime, I had also applied for a job in customer liaison for the Soft Drinks Industry, and was called for an interview at their offices in Upper Grosvenor Street, right by Hyde Park. It was a very pleasant part of the West End, near Marble Arch and the shopping delights of Oxford Street, and the work sounded reasonably interesting. I would be dictating letters to be sent to various people, either explaining the SDI's problems in wartime, or dealing with complaints from customers or retailers. It didn't sound like rocket science and carried a good salary, so I was delighted when they offered me the post, to start in two weeks time.

Buddy and I had discussed my plans to get a job, and she understood why I found it hard to settle down to life as a housewife. It would also be quite helpful for me to earn some money to add to her salary and the allowance I got from Ernest. We needed to find a really good day nursery for Paul, and, as she was the district nurse, she had some very useful contacts. Her enquiries bore fruit and we were offered a place in an excellent nursery, not far away, that was privately run and had a long waiting list. We had also agreed that Buddy would take Paul there in the morning, and collect him in the afternoon for the first few weeks, until I got used to making the journey to and from the West End.

Florence Avenue was almost opposite Enfield Chase Station, and at rush hour, the trains ran quite frequently to Kings Cross. From there, I could get a bus, or take the Tube, directly to Marble Arch, and it looked as though the journey would take just over an hour. Buddy would take Paul, who was a year old, to the nursery, on a child's seat fixed to the back of her bike, and we bought a little yellow mackintosh coat and sou'wester for him to wear when it rained. He looked adorable in it, so we were all set.

I hadn't expected rocket science, but the Soft Drinks Industry was technically quite complicated, and now it was necessary for me to understand how this particular cookie crumbled. I had always thought that lemonade was a fairly straight forward refreshing drink for hot summer days, or that tonic water went with gin, to help make a party enjoyable. I just didn't know anything about soft drinks. Some time later, when I more or less understood how the whole thing worked, and I wrote a parody of a Rupert Brooke poem, 'These I have loved'.

UNCON and CON, and PERMITS RECOMMENDED,

DECLARED RECEIPTS, RETURNS TO BE AMENDED,

The scarlet dash of GALLONAGE PERMITTED,

The pencil scrawl of COMP, deciphered by quick witted checkers,

Who tick, tick, from 9 till 5 (Can they really be alive?)

Unfortunately I can't remember any more, but the verse gives a taste of the complicated processes involved in regulating soft drinks in war time, and it was quite challenging to be part of the team which dealt with the outside world.

Most of the ingredients like sweetener, flavour and acid, were rationed and carbonation was also an issue. It seemed that only water, which is over 80% of the contents of any drink, came without needing a form to be filled in, or a request to be made. The SDI was protecting standards within the industry, and making sure that no 'cowboys' short-changed the paying public. They were anxious to stop the flooding of the market by any one product, and so 'permitted gallonage' was an important part of the system.

The office in Upper Grosvenor Street was 'open plan', and we worked within sight and sound of each other, which was fine, as the staff were all extremely pleasant. Most of the men had been rejected by one of the Forces for reasons of either health or age, and several of the women were typists who could turn their hands to general office work. The best thing, from my point of view, was that I found a new friend, Tim Jeremy, who kept me entertained if the day got a little tedious.

Tim was about fifteen years older than me, beautifully mannered and always immaculately dressed. He often wore a cravat instead of a tie, which actually looked very smart, and had a wonderfully modulated speaking voice, that made a very good impression on Buddy, when she met him. Early in our friendship, he told me that he was homosexual, which suited me beautifully as I was married, and he very soon became one of our closest friends. Paul was just a toddler, but Tim would play with him for hours and bought him some great toys. One Christmas, it was a little red train and coaches, all made of wood, and that became toy of the year in Florence Avenue.

Although I had always loved the theatre, my experience of either opera or ballet was extremely limited, and Tim set about putting that right, (shades of 'Educating Rita'). He took me to the Opera House in Covent Garden, with seats in the Grand Tier, and we saw 'Tosca', 'La Boheme' and one of the Wagner Ring cycle. Fortunately the government had controlled theatre prices, or he would have been quickly bankrupted. Then we went to ballet, with Margot Fonteyn and Frederick Ashton giving spectacular performances. We always ate out afterwards, and there was a controlled price meal at some of the smartest restaurants in town, so I had my first taste of both Chinese and Indian foods with Tim. Buddy was a wonderfully willing baby-sitter, and liked the fact that I was having fun with such a good friend, who was not a threat to Ernest.

Tim had a charming bed-sitting room in Hampstead and collected china, particularly 'famille rose', so I got to know quite a lot about porcelain, and the various patterns one could see in antique shops. He read a lot and particularly enjoyed the Sitwells, generously giving me copies of any books I said that I liked. I told him all about Ernest, hoping that they would become good friends when the war ended, and even took him to meet my Uncle Johnny, at his club, 'The Atheneum', in London. They got on very well together, though Uncle Johnny did most of the talking, and I was really, amused when Tim's goodbye was "It has been very enjoyable listening to you, sir!".

Paul seemed to enjoy having other toddlers to play with at the nursery, and our life in Enfield had settled down into a reasonably pleasant routine. Ernest had got as far as India with the West African Brigade, and as he was not involved in any action, I wrote lots of letters telling him about the things I was doing. I had joined an amateur dramatic society at Bush Hill Park, that called themselves the SWAN Players, (the 'Society Without A Name'), and played the character parts I always enjoyed. One member of the society, who liked to be the dramatic lead, was Stella, and an amazing thing happened in one scene, when she had to scream in fury in the middle of a quarrel. I was standing on stage and saw, as she started to shout, the top set of her false teeth fly out of her mouth. In a flash, her hand went up, caught them, and popped them back in place, She continued the scene, apparently undeterred, and, afterwards, was able to laugh about it, pleased that disaster had been averted.

The other staff at the SDI were very pleasant, and I was surprised, one day, to hear raised angry voices from across the office. Suddenly there was shocked silence and I wondered what on earth had happened.

Tim was nearby, so I whispered, "What is it?" "He used the bad word!" he said. I had no idea what he meant. "Do you mean 'damn'?" I inquired. He looked at me strangely, and said no, he meant the really bad word. "What's that?" I asked. He thought I was joking, and said,"Come on, Jay, you're twenty-five, don't try and tell me you haven't ever heard the word f....!" "F...?" I repeated, "I've never heard it before. "And I hadn't. Certainly not at the Convent, or in the Engineers' Office, or nursing in the army. No-one would ever have used that word in front of a woman, and in the end he believed me. It wasn't till I lived in New York City that I heard it again. Oh dear, how things were to change once the war was over.

Rationing was getting tighter every year and, ridiculously, the thing I missed most was chocolate. The meat ration was pathetically small, but we could eat fish, or eggs, if we could get them. The Ministry of Food was always publishing the most awful recipes that were supposed to make your mouth water, but I would have settled for a supply of Cadbury's Nut Milk Chocolate bars. Fruit, like whole bananas, were a thing of the past and oranges were rarely in the shops. Cherries, apples, pears and plums came into the market, in season, but all too quickly disappeared till the following year. Buddy had a big Bramley cooking apple tree in the garden, and there had been a beautiful cherry tree, until I had, accidentally, burnt it down, when I failed to put out a bonfire properly.

We had all kinds of tasteless things to eat: powdered egg, tinned meats, like spam and corned beef, and, for growing children and pregnant women, to give them Vitamin C, a concentrated orange juice, which I thought did not taste, one little bit, like oranges. We missed quite simple things like fresh eggs, and I shall never forget the gasp that came from the cinema audience when, in an American film, someone cooking breakfast, broke four lovely eggs into the frying pan. They looked absolutely mouth-watering, and much more desirable than caviar. Queuing became endemic. In fact, just to see a line of people waiting, meant something in short supply was on sale, and quite often we would join a queue at a shop, having no idea what we might be able to buy.

The war seemed to go on and on. Of course, we always followed the radio broadcasts of announcers, like Alva Liddell, who had told of the fighting in Russia and in Italy, but, suddenly, we heard the news everyone had been waiting for. The Allies were landing back in France, and in a final push, with huge casualties, the war ended on 8th May, 1945. Hitler had died in a bunker in Berlin and a wave of relief swept over the whole country, but for Ernest, stuck somewhere in the jungles of Burma, not a lot changed. The only consolation was that the Japanese could not hold out indefinitely on their own, but no-one knew how long it would take to force a surrender in the Far East.

The dropping of the atomic bomb on Hiroshima settled the matter in August, and by November, all fighting had stopped. We thanked heaven that it had not been necessary for the allies to invade Japan itself. Ernest was safe and would be coming home some time soon. In fact, he did not get back until July 1946, so for him, the war lasted almost seven years. He was nineteen when it started, and twenty-six when he finally came home.

The changes the war had made were vast and long lasting. From the Engineers' Office alone, Jim had died of cholera in Egypt; 'Dead', who had jumped over chairs rather than walk around them, had shrapnel lodged in his spine and would never walk again; Jack had a nervous breakdown after serving in North Africa, and the boss's son had died on the way to Dunkirk. I have no idea what became of the others, who may well have suffered equally dreadful fates.

In our little family, Dick, who had been taken prisoner at Dunkirk, was injured on the march to captivity and spent three years in a German prison camp. The injury led to his death several years later, when Peggy was declared, officially, a war widow. Ernest was physically uninjured, but he always said that his service in the army ruined his feet. More importantly, it certainly stole his youth, and he lost seven years in which he should have been carefree.

When, years later, the casualties became a statistic, it was thought that between four and five million people had died in the worst disaster in the history of mankind. We were, none of us, left unscathed by the Second World War.

Chapter 11

Once it was all too clear that it would take quite some time to bring the troops home from Burma and the Far East, we went back to the routine that we had grown used to in Enfield. Every day, Buddy took Paul to the nursery and I went on with my job in with the SDI. Tim was going to Stratford–upon–Avon, for a week in April, to see the RSC's latest productions, and he suggested that I might like to join him at the weekend, to see 'Hamlet'. I thought it was a great idea and, as Buddy agreed to look after Paul, I asked Tim to book a room for me at The Arden Hotel, and I would come by train on the Friday evening, straight from the office in London.

Although I had always loved Shakespeare, and had seen many of the plays over the years, starting from the Old Vic productions when I was still at school, I had never been to Stratford. It was a really exciting prospect, as there had been a big debate about the construction of the theatre, in the early thirties. Some critics had called the design, 'The Jam Factory', a concrete monstrosity on the banks of the beautiful Avon, while others defended the art deco square building as, 'modern' and 'fit for purpose'. I was ready to enjoy making up my own mind and knew that Tim would, doubtless, have strong views, one way or the other. As it happened, by the end of my stay, I couldn't have cared less about the aesthetics of theatre design, I was so carried away by the work that was being done on the stage.

Tim had already been there for a week and had found a group of actors who were great company off stage. Paul, John and Donald all had very good parts in the repertory of plays that were being performed by the

RSC. They were young and fun, and we had fascinating conversations after the performances, in the bar of the 'Black Swan', known to everyone as the 'Dirty Duck'. Tim was very taken with Donald, who went on to star, very successfully, in films in Hollywood. He was versatile and could play comedy or tragedy with equal finesse, very handsome and best of all, he was a delight to talk to.

Paul, who was playing Horatio in 'Hamlet', was different. He had a craggy face with scars from boyhood skin problems, but he was a brilliant actor, and he, too, went on to star in films in America, though his main fame came from his stage performances in England. He was married and had written a children's book which he had dedicated to his little son, and he, too, was a natural, unspoilt, amusing companion. The third actor, John, much quieter, but equally interesting, finally going on to become the Artistic Director at 'The West Yorkshire Playhouse' in Leeds, where I met up with him over forty years later.

Both Paul and Donald were eventually given knighthoods for 'services to the theatre', so though we didn't know it, we were in very exalted company. By the time I had spent three successive evenings with these wonderfully talented actors, I was ready to live in Stratford and spend the rest of my life in their company, but I couldn't quite see Ernest agreeing to the move.

The big event of the year was Ernest's return from Burma. It was an absolutely wonderful moment when he arrived in Enfield, not in uniform, but in his government-issue, demob suit. Nothing else seemed remotely important, and the shock of seeing him with a moustache, and looking slightly older, disappeared in the joy of having him safely back, for good. Buddy opened the bottle of champagne that she had saved for that moment and we were both very amused when Ernest described the army demob process. The suit was pretty ghastly, ill-fitting and shiny, but he was most put out that the size was labelled 'Portly'.

The hugging of his little son, now three, was a moment to savour, and thanks to the daily reminder of "Say goodnight to Daddy", Paul was delighted to have a real 'Daddy' back home. Tim came to Enfield to be introduced, and they seemed to get on very well, and Buddy was thrilled to have a man about the house, to make our lives complete. Everything looked rosy. The war was over, and our side had won. Ernest went back to Scotland Yard, in the Pensions' Department, to restart his Civil Service career as a clerical officer, and I continued at the SDI as though nothing had happened.

But, of course, something had happened. We were older. Ernest and I had both been very young when we were married, and we had 'grown up' apart. We had not spent enough time in each other's company to form the bonds that tie couples together. It really wasn't anyone's fault, and yet we were all culpable. The first problems, surprisingly, came with Paul. Ernest's absence and my job in London, had left Buddy in charge of her first grandchild. She was the one who saw most of him, and they loved each other dearly. Suddenly, a father, who perfectly naturally wanted to discipline and guide his little son, arrived on the scene. Inevitably, their interests clashed, and, as we lived in Buddy's house, tensions arose, and I was 'Piggy in the middle' of streams of constant bickering.

I actually felt that they were both being unreasonable, and as I loved them, it was not a good situation. Of course, at the SDI, there was Tim, who listened to my complaints about one or the other, and sympathised with my dilemma, but he was, wisely, careful to stay out of the struggle. Buddy had been head of the family since my father had died, and my main supporter through the war. Ernest had been far away for a long time, and wanted to take up the role of decision-maker in his own family. I had definitely changed from the nineteen year-old, who got engaged to him at the beginning of the war; and from the uncritical bride of three years later. This situation could not go on for long, and a crisis came when the three of us took a seaside holiday with Paul.

It was one of those silly little things that should have passed off without comment. We were on the beach late one afternoon, when Ernest told Paul to put away his bucket and spade as we were going back to our hotel for the evening. Paul, who was three, turned to Buddy and said that he didn't want to go, so Ernest took Paul's arm and told him to do as he was told. Buddy took his other arm and said he could stay with her. It was a real impasse, and no-one was coming out of it well. At this point

Paul started to cry, as Ernest and Buddy were holding on quite tightly. I was angry with both of them, and we all stormed back to the hotel, with a tearful little boy, and three furious grown-ups.

Although this particular argument blew over, it had made a big impression on me, and I couldn't see how the question of 'who was going to be boss?', was going to be solved. I tried talking to Buddy about the problem, but she pointed out that Ernest was often unreasonable, which was true, and the whole thing was not her fault. I got exactly the same response from Ernest. Living in the same house, they were definitely oil and water. My loyalties were divided and, to make matters worse, I felt responsible for many of the disagreements. I had changed and so had Ernest, and at that point I started wondering why on earth I had married him.

At the end of the war, I had begun to think that it might be a good idea for us to consider emigrating to one of the countries in the Empire, where opportunities for young families would be better than in war torn Britain. When Ernest got back from Burma, I had tried to talk to him about it but he wasn't interested. Perfectly reasonably, he said that he had had enough of the rest of the world and wanted to stay in England. Tim Jeremy thought South Africa might be a good place to live, while the £10 fare to Australia attracted me. I even went to Australia House in Trafalgar Square to find out what was involved, but it seemed that they were giving priority to skilled workers, or qualified professionals, like teachers and nurses My feet were definitely itching, but I could see little chance of making a permanent move anywhere.

The bickering between Buddy and Ernest continued non-stop, and I started to consider leaving them to sort things out for themselves. I thought that I might put Paul in a pre-prep boarding school, and look for a job abroad for a while. To my surprise, though he wouldn't discuss the idea, Ernest did not seem to be totally against it. Perhaps he could see that the status quo was not in anyone's interest, and would almost inevitably lead to the break-up of our marriage. I had always wanted to visit the United States, and so, selfishly, I made up my mind to try to do exactly that.

Once I had made the decision, it was like planning a gap year. First I needed a job, so I advertised in the personal column of The New York Times. I put something like 'Well-educated English woman, mid-twenties, seeks post in America, as companion or governess', or words to that effect! It brought a lot of answers, many of them proposing marriage or 'warm friendship'! There were several very sad replies, explaining that a woman had died and her husband needed someone to come and care for him and their children.

However, there was one response from a lawyer in New York that sounded just the sort of thing I was looking for. He had a wife and two children and they spent Thanksgiving in Oklahoma, Christmas in Florida, and the rest of the year in New York City. Mr McNulty's letter sounded business-like, and genuine. I studied a map and saw that it would be a wonderful chance to see very different parts of the USA. He was, obviously, well-off, and the children were Heather, who was four and a boy of six, named Dale. The family employed a cook-housekeeper, and my job would be to look after the children, who were not yet at school. I would be expected to teach them, and generally take care of them. It looked like the perfect temporary job, and one that I was fairly sure I could do well.

The main problem would be getting the immigration visa that would allow me to work, legally, in the United States. Mr M would have to take the responsibility of seeing that I did not become a charge on the state, and to show that he had the funds to support his claim. This would mean giving proof of his assets, which I thought he might not be ready to do, and I particularly did not want him to pay my fare, just in case I hated the job.

Surprisingly, all the paperwork went through without a hitch. My interview for the visa, at the American Embassy in Grosvenor Square, surprised me. They quite seriously asked, "Do you intend to try to overthrow the government of the United States of America?" The temptation to answer, "What a good idea!" was almost overwhelming, but I managed to shake my head, for I felt that the man behind the desk would not be keen on supposedly funny replies. Mr M made his promise to see that I wouldn't become a burden on the state, and the visa duly arrived.

I had found a very good boarding school for Paul, not far away, at Great Amwell, as he was now nearly four, and needed to begin his education. Strix, the principal, was committed to a pleasantly informal regime, where the children's happiness was of paramount importance. I would pay the fees, so that neither Ernest nor Buddy would be short of money, as the whole thing was my idea. The school was in a lovely old building that had once been a manor house. It was surrounded by woodland that was covered in bluebells in the spring and the lawns had huge, spreading cedars that the children were allowed to climb.

'Pinewood School' was not too far from the railway station at Ware, so it was easy to get to, and the Greenline bus stop was at the end of the driveway. I liked the staff that I met on my first visit, and I thought it would be good for Paul to be with other children of his own age. Many of the parents were working outside the UK, so the school holidays were not a problem, as lessons stopped but care continued. Certainly the pupils came from a wide variety of home backgrounds, from successful actors to African diplomats, and I thought that Paul would be happy there.

By a very lucky chance, the headmistress-owner, Strix, was in need of someone who could help with the massive amounts of paperwork that were involved in running a private school. Ernest liked her, so when she suggested that, if he needed somewhere to live while I was away, he could stay at the school in return for clerical assistance. He jumped at the idea. It was a perfect temporary solution. He would be with Paul, able to keep an eye on him, but free to enjoy a new-found bachelor status, if he wanted to. I think he understood why I was going away for a while, and that, if our marriage was to survive, someone had to do something pretty drastic.

Buddy was less easy to satisfy. She hated the whole scenario. The fact that Paul would no longer be at home, made her reject the whole plan, even though she would be able to see him as often as she liked. She had always been very good at emotional blackmail, and I got the full force of it, unremittingly. One morning she tripped slightly on the stairs and I reminded her that this was supposed to be a sign one would soon be married. She raised her hand, dramatically, to her forehead and moaned, "Buried, more likely!". However, I went ahead with my plans and hoped they would turn out well in the end.

When term began, at the beginning of September, I had hired a pony and trap for us to drive Paul to his new school, in style. Buddy had finally accepted that I really was going to America, and was satisfied with my promise that I would be back within a year. The journey to Great Amwell kept her busy, as the pony was quite keen to hurry on, and she was in control of getting us there safely. When we arrived, still in one piece, we were shown the comfortable dormitory where Paul would sleep, and we went around the lovely gardens and the stables which were attached to the side of the house. We said goodbye to Strix and then quietly slipped away while Paul was playing with some other children. The journey back to Enfield in the pony and trap was less traumatic than I had feared, as Buddy realised that Ernest would be joining Paul at Pinewood as soon as I had left, and that she could easily take the Greenline bus from Enfield, to visit them at weekends.

I had resigned from the SDI, and paid for a one way, tourist class ticket to New York on Cunard's transatlantic liner, the Queen Elizabeth, leaving on 11th October. The plan was that Mr M would meet the ship when she docked, and I would spend a night in the city, before taking the two day train journey to Tulsa, in Oklahoma, where Mrs M would collect me from the station. I started to feel like a parcel.

Both Ernest and Buddy came to Waterloo to see me off. I tried to be cheerful, though, when I thought about it, I was taking a huge risk. Suppose I hated the job, or the people? I knew absolutely no-one in America, had little or no money, and there would be no friends to turn to if anything went wrong. What if little Paul got ill, or had an accident? Buddy had suggested that, once I had gone, a handsome chap like Ernest would find other women, and I would have lost my husband, but I told her that if his love would fade so easily, perhaps it was as well to let it go. Despite our disagreements, I knew I would miss them both tremendously.

The train for Southampton was waiting when we arrived at the station, and I got into a 'Ladies Only' carriage, with my trunk. I gave each of them a big kiss and a hug, and waved as the whistle blew and the train steamed out on to the main line. I was crying, and so were they, for I was about to leave England on a ship bound for the U.S.A. !

Chapter 12

The Cunard liner, 'Queen Elizabeth', was huge. She seemed to fill the dock in Southampton, and I could see virtually nothing else, except a vast panorama of lifeboats, portholes, decks and railings. She towered above the quayside and seemed to go on and on, upwards into the sky. Once I had gone through the Customs' sheds and had my passport and my ticket checked, I walked up the gangway on to the ship. After years of forced austerity in wartime, it was almost incredible to step into flamboyant luxury, and it felt totally unreal, as if I was in a Hollywood film.

The QE had been used as a troop and hospital ship during the war and had been totally refitted, with no expense spared. Now the brilliant colours of the décor, the sparkle of shining metal, and the carpeted expanse of sweeping staircases made the wonderful liner tremendously impressive, and I was suitably amazed. I was travelling in tourist class, the least expensive, so my cabin was on one of the lower decks, but it seemed perfectly comfortable, and I was dying to explore the ship, once she had set sail.

For the moment, I went up on deck and listened to the band on the quay playing a farewell medley, and ships' hooters sounding from all around us. Many of the visitors had come to goodbye parties on board, and had only left when the "All ashore, who are going ashore!" announcement was made. They were now waving from the dock, as the tugs started nosing the huge bulk of the Queen Elizabeth, out into the Solent. The band struck up, 'Will ye no come back again?' and this, I realised, was the point of no return. I determined to be positive, and to make the most of my time in America, when I got there. Meantime, I meant to enjoy the voyage across the Atlantic in this beautiful ship.

Though the QE took less than a week to reach New York, it was a memorable crossing. The food was unbelievable. I couldn't remember eating so many delicious things before, and that was in the 'tourist class'. What it must be like in the 'first class' restaurant I couldn't imagine. The separation of classes, seemed to be very carefully preserved, which was hardly surprising, as it probably cost about four times as much to travel first class. The doors that led from one section to another were always guarded, but this didn't worry me, as I felt lucky to be on the ship at all.

In 1947, if you wanted to travel to the United States, for either business or pleasure, you went by sea. There were no cheap flights, and the Atlantic crossing was a wonderful source of revenue to a country just recovering from a major war. 'The Blue Riband' was a much sort-after accolade, with such ships as the Mauretania competing in the effort to cut down the time it took to cross the ocean. Cunard ran a regular service between Southampton and New York, and the Queen Mary and the Queen Elizabeth proved their worth, carrying film stars, politicians and famous faces of all kinds, in luxury and comfort. Only much later, when air travel took over, did the two Queens become cruise ships, as well as trans-Atlantic liners.

There were lots of things to do. Deck games like shuffle board, tournaments for table tennis, and always plenty of people to chat to. I definitely enjoyed the social life of the ship, and joined in everything I possibly could. One particularly enjoyable evening, was the 'horse racing' that involved a great deal of energy on the part of the passenger 'jockeys'. The tourist purser, a very likeable young chap, with blue eyes and gingery hair, whose name was Dickinson, usually ran the games. He chose me to be his favoured passenger, which was very flattering and great fun. Dickie and I became close friends, so I was sad that the crossing only took five days. I really liked him, and when he suggested that we could meet in New York next time the QE docked there, it seemed a pity that this would not be possible. I told him that I would be in Oklahoma, hundreds of miles away, but he seemed so sure that we could have great fun together that I promised that I would let him know, via Cunard's New York office, if and when I came back to the east coast.

Being Dickie's friend, literally opened doors on the ship. He took me dancing in the First Class ballroom, and he looked wonderful in his blue mess kit, though I noticed that he drank gin at every opportunity. We lived in the present. I didn't ask him about his home in England, and he didn't ask me. It was, I thought, a case of ships that passed in the night, and we just enjoyed each other's company. Certainly, he made the voyage great fun for me!

Every so often a bowl of delicious fruit, or a bunch of flowers would materialise on the little table in my cabin, and I began to think that I had a secret admirer on board. I looked around for any sign of a handsome Romeo casting longing glances in my direction, but, whoever he was, he remained obstinately invisible. I asked Dickie how I could find out who the generous donor was, and he was very amused by the whole idea. It seemed that I was a 'recommended passenger', and the bounty was straight out of the ship's stores. Although I had paid my own fare, Mr M had made the actual booking with Cunard, and had had to pull strings to get me a cabin. Someone important had put in a word for me, so I was deemed to be worthy of little extras. I came down to earth with a bump.

All too soon, it was the final night and I had to pack my trunk ready for the next day's challenge. Dickie and I danced till the early hours, and the orchestra chose really nostalgic tunes that were right for the occasion, as we waltzed across the ballroom for the final time. Songs like 'Who's taking you home tonight?', were especially poignant, as for many of the passengers it was the end of a lovely shipboard romance, and the real world would soon be crowding in on them. Dickie and I finished the evening with a promenade in the moonlight along the open deck. We leant on the railings and watched the sea stream by, sparkling with reflected light. We promised to keep in touch, exchanged goodbye kisses and I went to my cabin, ready to face the next day.

The ship came in sight of the sensational form of the Statue of Liberty in the early afternoon, and my first impression of New York was truly memorable. Although I had never been there before, the films had made the skyline so familiar and so reassuring, that I felt I already knew the city. As we slowly steamed up the East River, darkness began to fall and the towering skyscrapers lit up, one by one. The reflections of car headlights and the red and green of the traffic lights, mixed in with the street lamps that ran like chains of pearls across the bridges, gave an enchantment that must have seemed like a miracle to the 'huddled masses', if they had survived the journey to the New World. I was sure I was going to like life in the United States, and I wrote quick postcards to both Ernest and Buddy to send them my love and say that I had arrived safely

Disembarkation was fairly straightforward, at least it seemed so. Porters took the cases to the Customs' sheds, where they could be claimed by the owner and taken off to waiting taxis. I showed my passport, complete with visa, to the immigration authorities, and almost immediately located my trunk among the stacks of other people's luggage. I got a porter to take it through the shed, and I was not unduly perturbed when the uniformed Customs' officer asked me to unlock and open it. I expected a quick glance at the neatly folded clothes, before he marked it with the magic chalk tick that meant all clear to leave.

No such luck! I never found out why, but they thoroughly searched through all my worldly possessions. The official took absolutely everything out of the trunk, until the whole bench was piled with my clothes, and looked exactly like a table at a jumble sale. When the trunk was completely empty he felt all around the lining, apparently searching for secret pockets where small items could have been hidden. Finally, almost reluctantly, he picked up his chalk stick, marked the trunk with the necessary symbol, and strolled off to his next victim. I was left to try to put everything back, in some kind of order, find a porter, and go on to the exit gate at the end of the dock, to try to find Mr M, my new employer.

He was waiting there, getting worried. Everyone else had left and I think it may have crossed his mind that, once the ship had docked,

I could have done a runner! After all I had my visa, and in a very big country it might have been difficult to catch me, if I chose to disappear. I apologised for the long delay and told him about the search of my belongings, which he said was very unusual. There must have been a tip-off that some smuggling was about to take place, and as I was on an immigration visa, I was a natural suspect. However, he was clearly relieved to see me and said that we would have dinner before he dropped me off at the hotel, where I was to spend the night.

He picked up my trunk and we walked into a side street where his big American car was parked. He put my luggage on the back seat, and, as we drove away, I got a good look at him. He was totally unmemorable, of medium height and stocky build, and he had obviously not dressed-up for the occasion, as he was wearing a rather crumpled tweed suit. His curly auburn-brown hair had started to thin, and his complexion was rather florid. I noticed that his eyes were brown and quite close set, which gave him a rather mean look, but he seemed perfectly pleasant and I decided to withhold judgement as to whether I liked him or not.

He took me for a drive to look at the city, and it was tremendously impressive. The huge advertisement for Marlborough cigarettes immediately caught my eye, as gigantic smoke rings swirled across above our heads. The changing neon signs in every shape and colour I could think of, flashed irregularly on and off, and the theatres and cinemas were alight with names and titles. I was, finally, on Broadway.

Mr M parked the car in a back street, and we took the short walk to the restaurant where we were to have dinner with one of his friends, an American senator, who had been involved in the 'Lease-Lend' programme, during the war. The senator waiting for us had rimless glasses and looked like a rather sprightlier Franklin D. Roosevelt. His very deep voice boomed through the restaurant like a ship's hooter and he referred to me throughout as 'The Little English Girl'. Everyone within earshot was left in no doubt about where I'd come from.

They ordered for me, which was fine, and the waiter brought the biggest platter of food I'd ever seen. It was called 'A Blue Plate Special' and it looked like dinner for four. There was a roast chicken, a pile of mushrooms, several baked tomatoes and a huge portion of what I would have called chips, and they referred to as 'French fries'. I gasped, and said that it looked rather a lot, but they just laughed and then proceeded to take things off their plates and put them on mine, with a jolly, "You try this....", which was extremely embarrassing. Fortunately, they soon forgot I was there, and they went on to an animated discussion about Senator this, that, and the other, who had been in trouble, or was about to be, any minute now. They dropped names right, left and centre, and I could see that Mr M, whom I knew was a lawyer, was fairly heavily into political shenanigans of one kind or another.

It was nearly nine o'clock by the time we went back to the car, the Senator keeping us company, but we were in for a nasty surprise. My luggage had disappeared from the back seat. There was no sign of a forced entry into the car, and Mr M was very quick to protest that he remembered locking the door earlier, so the thieves, he said, must have picked the lock.. The fact remained that my trunk had gone, and, with it, everything I owned. All my clothes, washing things, make-up, photos of home, souvenirs of the cruise, had been stolen, and I was, literally, left with the clothes I stood up in. Fortunately my passport was in my handbag, but I had no other hand luggage. I really didn't know what to do.

The Senator sprang into action at once, and told Mr M that we must go immediately to the local precinct to report the theft, so we did. Even in the horror of the situation, I couldn't help noting that the police station looked exactly like the ones on the films. What was more, so did the police officers. I filled in a form that registered my loss, and answered questions like, "Do you remember seeing your case on the seat when you left the car?", as if perhaps, absentmindedly, I might have taken a heavy trunk to the restaurant and left it there. No-one seemed to think it would be found, so the reality of the situation was horribly clear. I had no night clothes, no washing things, nothing! For the first time since I left England, I felt a long way from home.

Of course, a temporary solution had to be found, so leaving the Senator muttering apologies to the poor little English girl for the harsh treatment she had received from the criminal element in New York City, Mr M found a drugstore that was still open at midnight. He watched me chose washing things, a nightie and a change of underwear, promising to see I was fully recompensed for my loss at some future date, paid the bill and drove me to my over-night hotel. My room was on the 22nd floor, which was the highest I'd ever been in any building, and when I looked out of the window, the street looked miles below, and the cars tiny. I had a terrible desire to throw something like a glass of water down on to them.

Surprisingly, I slept like a top in my new drugstore nightdress, had coffee and a doughnut for breakfast, and was ready when Mr M came to take me to the railway station. Grand Central was really impressive, crowded with people, noisy, and with that indefinable smell of steam trains. I was given my ticket, one way to Tulsa, and it had a number that would tell me where my bunk was. I shook hands with Mr M, and went up the steep little flight of steps, into the train. Once again, it was like the movies, and this time I was en route to cowboy country, to the best known state in all the world. The steam engine let out a short series of hoots, and with lots of chuffs and clanks it pulled the long train out of the station, and we started the journey. It was to be "Oh, Oklahoma!"

Chapter 13

The inside of the train was an eye-opener. It was just like a hotel, with all the amenities for quite long stays, and as it made its way past the outer suburbs of New York, I went to find where I would be sleeping for the next two nights. The journey to Tulsa would take nearly three days, and though I had seen the 'wagons-lits' in films, I was amazed at how big the berths looked. My number was in the upper section, and I wondered how on earth I could get up to it. I looked around, but the only way seemed to be by climbing up the face of the lower bunk, and then swinging over the guard rail that ran along the side. With a great deal of puffing and panting, I successfully landed on the coverlet and leant back on the pillows. It was beautifully comfortable, and I decided to have a short rest, before I continued my exploration of the rest of the carriages. There were little curtains along the open side, that could be closed to give privacy when night came, and the gentle rocking of the train made me certain that I would sleep well.

At this point I thought I should find out where the washrooms were, so I swung back over the guard rail to start my descent to the floor of the carriage. I was just carefully negotiating the final drop of about five feet, and wondering how on earth older people could manage to get down from the top bunks, when a voice came from behind me, "What you-all doin', ma'am?" It was a black uniformed conductor, peering at me in amazement. I made the last bit of the descent, and then turned to explain that I was just getting down from my sleeping berth, which I thought was quite a difficult manoeuvre. His response was to point to a button beside the top bunk, that had the printed instruction, 'Ring to call the conductor.' I hadn't even noticed it. Apparently, he would then bring a portable ladder that would make the ascent or descent quite simple and considerably more dignified.

A further exploration of the train revealed an observation car, where you could sit and have a drink, as you watched America whiz by, a very pleasant restaurant carriage, and rows of upholstered arm chairs, which looked perfect for reading or just looking out of the window. I had settled comfortably in one, when I was joined by a jolly group of three salesmen, returning to Texas from a sales' conference in New York. They were intrigued to meet someone from England, and I went through the first of many requests to "Say something, in that wonderful accent!" that anyone who has visited the United States will recognise all too well.

I said quite a lot, trying to find out what Oklahoma was like, but they didn't know. They were from Texas, and they said they worked for "Joskeys, the largest store in the largest state!" They were fascinatingly Texan, and carefully pulled up their trouser legs to show me the ornately carved handles of the vicious looking knives that were tucked into the top of their high-heeled cowboy boots. They plied me with a drink I had never had before, 'Rum and Coke', in large paper cups, and everything got very happy, and we all laughed a lot. They took me to dinner that evening in the restaurant car, and the food was delicious. They had huge chunks of steak, served with 'French fries' and big side salads, followed by apple pie, 'à la môde', which turned out to mean, with ice cream, so I stopped wondering why they were all rather chubby. When I finally said goodnight, leaving them to finish their supply of rum, I found my way back to the sleeping car and after a quick wash, called for the conductor to bring the ladder. I changed into my nightie in the bunk, behind closed curtains, put my head on the pillow and fell asleep.

The next day I met the Texans again and they had decided that I should abandon the idea of Oklahoma, and go on with them to Texas. They would find work for me at Joskeys, and I could stay with their families until I found somewhere to live. It was a kind thought but, as I explained to them, I had accepted the job in Oklahoma, and I was going to keep my promise. At St Louis, the train divided into two parts, one for Oklahoma and the other for Texas, so we parted company with good wishes both ways, and they went happily back to Houston, ready to report on their impressions of the New York sales' conference.

The Oklahoma portion of the train waited for two hours at St Louis, so I thought there was a chance to take a look at the Mississippi, with its Huckleberry Finn connections, which ran through the city. I found the river quite easily, as it was very wide, though a disappointing greyish-brown colour, moving only sluggishly along. I turned to go back to the station and suddenly realised that I had no idea in which direction to walk. There was a police officer directing traffic, so I went over and asked the way to the railway station.

At first, my English accent threw him, but finally he understood the question, and asked which station I wanted, as there were three. I had passed a large ornate fountain as I left the train, so I said, "The one with the fountain outside it." He was totally puzzled. I could have been speaking in a foreign language. "The what?" he queried, so I said it again. No better, so I started to describe the fountain, with water thrown up into the air, and then falling down into a big basin. He got the hang of it straight away, "Ah, you mean a fantn.", and to my relief, (and, I suspect, his), he was able to answer my question. Fortunately it wasn't too far away, and I got back to the train with several minutes to spare.

The rest of the journey went by without incident, and I watched the prairies flash by, green and flat, so that you could see for miles. The train finally pulled into the station at Tulsa, and, by then, I was quite ready to meet Mrs M and the children. It wasn't difficult to spot the little family who were waiting for me, and I thought they looked very pleasant. Mrs M was tall and elegant, Dale looked quite big for six, and Heather, only four, was a very pretty little girl, with lovely fair hair. We went to the car, which looked extremely expensive, and Mrs M sympathised with the loss of my suitcase in New York, promising that we could go shopping, where they lived, to replace at least some of the clothes I had lost.

The children were slightly overawed at meeting someone with a funny English accent, so they were quite quiet in the back seat of the car, but Mrs M and I chatted about life in Oklahoma, as we drove the thirty or so miles back to Cleveland. She told me that she had been born in the mid-west, and that her father had been an oil man. She always spent Thanksgiving in Oklahoma, as they had cousins living just over the Arkansas border, about sixty miles away, and there was an annual family reunion. Mr M was a lawyer in New York, but he would be coming down to spend Thanksgiving with the family, in Cleveland. They had a big apartment in Manhattan, and a house in Palm Beach, in Florida, as well as the one we were driving to, and she was sure I would enjoy seeing such very different parts of the country.

When we reached Cleveland, it turned out to be a really small town. There was a sign, as we drove in, telling the visitor that there were one thousand, two hundred and twenty-one inhabitants, and I could see that there was a single main street, with ribbon development on either side. I spotted a good selection of small shops, a couple of cafés and a little cinema, before we turned into a side road. Most of the houses, so far, seemed to have been built of wood, but now I saw what, in an English village, might have been the Manor House. It stood, in its own grounds, brick built and surrounded by a wire fence. We pulled into the front driveway, and I was suitably impressed. When Mrs M opened the heavy front door, I could see a spacious hallway and a wide staircase. Dale and Heather ran on, telling me to come and see my bedroom, so I followed them up the stairs to a corridor with several rooms leading off it, one of which was mine.

I supposed it had been a guest room, as they hadn't had a 'governess' before, and it was comfortable and well furnished. There was a big double window with a good view of the huge lawned garden, which had some beautiful trees. When I asked what they were, Dale told me they were pecans, (which he pronounced 'per-carns'), and that they had delicious nuts on them. As I absolutely loved nuts, I made a mental note to try one at the first opportunity. Mrs M called us to come down to have dinner, so the children led me down the stairs to a very big dining room, with a massive table, that clearly seated at least eight, and we sat down to a delicious meal.

They obviously had a very good cook, because the food was superb, but to my surprise both children rejected everything they were offered.

All they wanted was "Apple-cart juice!", which I thought was a, rather cute, American children's name for apple juice. This charming idea was quickly dispelled when Mrs M went out to the kitchen and came back with a carton clearly labelled 'Apricot Juice'. I decided that one thing I would try to do, would be to get Dale and Heather to realise how lucky they were to have such delicious things to eat. I also planned to be careful or, after years of rationing in England, I would soon get VERY fat.

I started at once being a 'governess'. They had reading books and we worked on them for at least an hour every day. We did simple sums, and I taught them songs and nursery rhymes. A big atlas showed them the different countries in Europe, and as Dale remembered the war, they heard about that too. We made scrapbooks, and pressed flowers and leaves, and Heather, who could already print her name, learnt joined up writing. In our 'schoolroom', an unused room on the top corridor, we did lessons and played board games like 'Snakes and Ladders', while in the garden we played hit and run with tennis balls, as Dale loved baseball. It was all purposeful and enjoyable, but I was struck by the fact that they really didn't seem to know how to 'play', for any length of time.

The problem was solved by a lucky chance. A friend of Mrs M's offered her an old pony, called 'Boyo' that had been used on a ranch to help round-up cattle. Would the children like to have it to ride, as it was in a field on its own and needed someone to love it. Would the children like it ? They certainly would, if I had anything to do with it. The field was quite near, so we all trooped round to have a look at Boyo. He was a lovely chestnut, old enough to be docile, but young enough to enjoy trotting round the field with someone riding bareback.

The next morning we took our lessons in the field with Boyo, and then we all rode round the field, several times, to make sure that he was as quiet to ride as he seemed to be. It was huge fun, with possibilities for make-believe that were endless, and by the end of the week our play had metamorphosed into full-blown drama. We took a big blanket and some poles from the garden of the house, and made a tee-pee. Matches and kindling started a camp fire, and we cooked sausages in an old frying pan. Dale was the brave warrior, Heather, the lovely Indian princess and

I was the old squaw who did the cooking, and kept on having to ride round the field to get supplies for the warrior and the princess.

Dale wore a Red Indian feathered headdress when he went out hunting buffalo, Heather had a shawl to make her look regal, while the old squaw just had some cowboy trousers with chaps, to let her do her riding in comfort! The days became so enjoyable that the children said they didn't want Thanksgiving to come, because once that was over, we were all going on to Florida. I was pleased that our tee-pee cooking was all eaten-up, and they got hungry enough to enjoy the delicious meals that we had in the dining room. We made-up stories and sang songs round our fire, and when we got back to the house, Dale and Heather told their mother the day's adventures, before they went to bed and slept like tops.

Mr M duly arrived for Thanksgiving, and he had to hear all about the exciting days with Boyo, though he didn't seem very anxious to listen to more than a brief description. I'm sure he loved his children, but he wanted peace and quiet and not the rattle of little tongues. The Thanksgiving dinner was absolutely delicious. Roast turkey with all the trimmings, followed by the most wonderful pudding I had ever eaten. 'Pumpkin pie' literally melted in your mouth, with a taste of cinnamon in the soft, sweet filling. It was memorable. We took Mr M to see Boyo in the field, and the warrior and the princess showed off their bareback riding skills, which he appreciated as he was a keen horseman himself. The following day, we all went to visit the cousins over the Arkansas border, and I was surprised that we didn't set off till after lunch. It seemed that the sixty miles we had to travel over dirt roads to get there wasn't far, and we just went for tea.

The Mullendore cousins lived in a magnificent house, with a working ranch attached, and were, clearly very rich. It was 'oil money' that the grandfather had made when he struck lucky as a prospector. They were, also, very proud to tell me that their grandmother had been a full-blown Red Indian. I knew nothing about the history of Oklahoma, so they were delighted to explain that the government had ceded the land to the native Indians, in perpetuity, as somewhere for the tribes to live, after they had been conquered by the invading settlers. It was not a generous gift, as it was thought to be a particularly poor area that was of little use to anyone. However, the discovery of oil changed all that, the land was taken back, and the tribes driven off elsewhere. As a sop to Cerberus, the American government agreed to give money from the oil revenue to the tribes and their successors in perpetuity, so the family still received an annual income, as their share of the largesse.

After tea, the cousins asked if I would like to meet some real cowboys, and when I enthusiastically said I would, they told their boy of nine, who was called E.C., to take me to see the 'bunkhouse'. Dale and Heather came too, and he led us to a huge barn attached to the house. I looked around for the cowboys, but it seemed we had to pretend to go by car, so we all piled into one that was parked ready for use. E.C. took the wheel, and I made appropriate brruum-brruum noises, to join in the game. To my total horror, EC quite confidently started the engine, and we drove out of the barn. I shouted at him to stop, but we drove on for about half a mile till we came to a very big building, just off the road. I was still getting over the shock of being driven by a nine year old boy, when a pleasant young chap came out to the car, and welcomed us to the bunkhouse.

It was a large barn that looked very basic. There were bunks along the sides, in two tiers, a bare table and several chairs, a sort of giant bed-sitter for a group of chaps. Lolling around were some young men, wearing plaid shirts, cowboy boots and shabby cowboy hats. They had obviously never met anyone English before, and they gave me the once over, as if I was a maverick steer that had unexpectedly joined the herd. Gary Cooper, they were not. I asked one of them what they did in their free time, expecting stories of parties in the wagons, or lassoing contests. He told me, shyly, that they went into town, about twenty miles away, to see a movie, and when I asked what kind of films they enjoyed, I was not unduly surprised to hear that their favourites were westerns.

On our way back to Cleveland, I asked Mrs M if she realised that E.C. drove the car around, which I thought was quite dangerous, because he could barely see over the steering wheel. Of course, she did know, and volunteered the information that he drove his sister to school every day. The family owned so much land that he never had to go on any public roads. I made a mental note to learn to drive in the near future. It couldn't be very difficult, if a boy of nine could do it.

Our time in Oklahoma was coming to an end and I had really enjoyed the mid-west in the autumn. I had even taken walks around the fields near the house, until someone congratulated me on being so 'courageous'. It seemed that there were a lot of rattlesnakes locally, with the power to bite and kill intruders. My career as a rambler ended abruptly, at that moment.

Chapter 14

In early December, the family moved from chilly winds and the first flurries of snow in Oklahoma, to the blue skies and warm sun of Florida. Palm Beach, on the Atlantic coast, was a very expensive haven for the rich and famous. I knew that their house would be luxurious, but so was every other one in the neighbourhood. I wrote to Ernest to give him the new address, and couldn't resist telling him about the coconut palms that grew everywhere. The autumn hurricane season was over, but the result of the winds was a harvest of the huge outer casings of coconuts around the base of every tree. I was really excited and, much to everyone's amusement, I quickly picked up as many as I could carry.

I took one into the big kitchen to try to cut away the outside, which proved to be very difficult, but finally, on the table, I had before me, a wonderful 'fairground' nut. I borrowed a hammer to split it open and enjoyed the milk inside, before cutting off wedges of deliciously moist, white chewy coconut. I knew there were hundreds more, just waiting to be picked up, and I could hardly wait. Of course, I very soon tired of eating them, and they lay around everywhere, slowly splitting open with sprouting roots and new little tufts of greenery. Coconuts had seemed so much more attractive, when they were in short supply. Let that be a lesson to us all!

The house in Palm Beach was very comfortably furnished, with four big bedrooms leading off a long first floor corridor. Mr and Mrs M had a beautiful room, with its own bathroom, and huge windows overlooking the garden. Dale and Heather shared a front bedroom and I had one at the back of the house, which left a spare room for guests. Downstairs the 'living room', as they called it, was huge, with an impressive fireplace for chilly evenings, if they ever came, and wide window seats that looked very countrified, The massive sofas were soft and inviting, and the floor was covered in a variety of thick-piled rugs. Next to it, the dining room had a long table and eight chairs, and I imagined that there might be dinner parties once we had settled down for the winter.

The garden had some of the loveliest flowers I had ever seen, and I was amazed that they all called it 'the yard', which, in England would have been a little space at the back of a house, with a dustbin as its main feature. On the first day I saw a beautiful red bird on a branch, and hurried in to see if we should try and catch it, as I was sure it had escaped from an aviary. They all came out to look and explained that it was a red cardinal, and a native of Florida. I had a lot to learn.

There was no pool in the garden, but 'The Bath and Tennis Club' was within easy walking distance and the Mc Nultys had a family membership, so we could go there whenever we liked. It was terribly smart, but had a lovely sandy beach where the children and I could sit, as we did our lessons. The fun with 'Boyo' in Cleveland, was replaced by writing in the sand and swimming in the club's pool, in gloriously warm weather. I got a very good tan, perhaps a little too good, as several people thought I might be partly coloured, which, in the USA in 1948, was not a social advantage.

Buses still had seats for white people, separated from the seats for coloureds, and it was surprisingly easy to get used to being one of the privileged ones. I used to take the bus into West Palm Beach on my day off, and go to see the greyhound racing at the popular dog track. West Palm Beach was a totally different town, and there were a lot of Spanish-speaking people working in the shops. The whole place was nothing like as exclusive as Palm Beach, where the only black faces you ever saw, belonged to the domestic staff.

The Dog Track was great fun, and I could never resist just a little gamble to complete the excitement. Before a race there was a buzz of noise and anticipation as the dogs were put into their starting boxes, and last minute bets placed. I played the numbers, since I didn't know anything about the racing form of the runners, and the two outside dogs, numbers five and six, carried my dollars. They started the hare well behind the line of dogs, and the sung chant, "Here comes the bun-ny!" on a rising inflection, came as it passed the dog boxes, and opened the gates. Greyhounds definitely enjoy chasing hares, and the spectators' adrenalin flowed as we all shouted in support of our chosen dog. All too soon the race would be over, the runners parading for the next one, and my betting slip torn up and put in the bin. I can only remember winning once, but that was a wonderful feeling of success that made up for all the past disappointments.

Money was short as I was getting a mere hundred dollars a month, which I soon realised was well below the going rate, but as my only expenses were trips on my days off, I didn't try to get a raise. Christmas came about three weeks after we arrived from Oklahoma, and I was interested to see what would happen in Florida. My first surprise came when I asked Dale and Heather what presents they planned to give to their parents, and when they wanted me to take them to do the shopping. They were genuinely amazed at the idea. I had it all wrong. Children didn't give to parents - it was the other way round! I told them that, in England, you always gave something to your mother and father, so that's what we would do this year, and they must save some of their pocket money to buy a little gift. They mustn't tell anyone, it was our Christmas secret.

I thought it would be fun for them to do a Christmas show for their parents, so I taught them 'Away in a manger', and found a little poem in a children's book that they could recite and act out.

"Santa Claus is on his way to greet you all on Christmas Day. His Christmas sack has such a load, it's spilling playthings on the road, Dolls and drums, all sorts of toys, for wishful little girls and boys, But still he has a lot to spare, for Christmas stockings, everywhere. And, as he hastens on his way, his sleigh bells carol out to say A MERRY CHRISTMAS ON THIS DAY!"

They could soon perform it, with lots of dramatic mime, and then, as a finale, sing 'Away in a manger'. I cut out little collars from white card and they wore them around their necks, like two little choirboys. We planned on performing the show for their parents, before they got up on Christmas morning, and at the same time, present the cards the children had made, and the gifts they had bought.

It all went well, and everyone was absolutely delighted, both with the entertainment and the unexpected gifts. Unfortunately, Mr M liked it so much that whenever anyone came to the house, the children were called on to do their 'piece', and, by about the tenth time, they were bored with the whole thing, which was a great pity. However, the house was beautifully decorated with a spectacular tree, and it did seem like Christmas. I thought about Ernest, Paul and Buddy, who were spending the holiday at Florence Avenue, and desperately wished I could have joined them for a big family hug. I was determined that, all being well, we would spend the following Christmas together in England.

Once the New Year was over, the children and I settled down to a pleasant routine in Palm Beach. We spent the day with lessons at the Bath and Tennis Club, eating lunch in the restaurant there, and got back to the house for tea, some games, evening dinner and then bedtime. The cook produced the most mouth-watering pancakes in huge stacks, with maple syrup and butter, and I could see myself getting fatter by the day. A sweet tooth is not a good thing to have if you are trying to diet, and any pathetic attempts I made to avoid fattening meals, fell to pieces when I nibbled innumerable Hershey Bars. I got a shock when, for the first time in my life, I weighed ten stone. I had put on a stone since I sailed on the Queen Elizabeth five months earlier.

The weather in Florida, in the winter, was fantastic. We had the odd shower, when the skies opened in a brief monsoon, but nearly every morning started with clear blue skies and bright sunshine, that lasted all day. The climate was wonderful for citrus fruits, and orange, grapefruit and lemon trees seemed to be growing everywhere I looked. For quite a long time I found it really exciting to go up to a tree and pick an orange. They tasted totally different from the ones we had bought in Enfield, for it seemed that fruit, picked for export, was not allowed to ripen on the tree, or it would have been rotten by the time it reached the markets of the world. The oranges and grapefruit I picked in the garden in Palm Beach, were fully ripe, sweet, juicy and totally delicious.

Commercial fruit growing had brought prosperity to Florida, and the winter advent of the 'Snowbirds', visitors from the northern states, had led to a huge increase in the number of houses that had been built. We all went in the car to Miami, and I was amazed to find that it was a really big city, with exciting art deco buildings, and a lot of bars and night clubs. We went into one shop where all the assistants spoke in Spanish, and Mrs M thought they could be Mexican migrant workers, many of whom were in the United States illegally. I was getting used to prices in dollars instead of pounds, and, as the exchange rate made a dollar worth five shillings, I had to do a great deal of mental arithmetic before I bought anything.

The war had been over for less than two years, but people were already starting to invest in new homes and new cars, giving a boost to the economy. The allied nations owed big debts to the USA for the food and arms that had made victory possible, so it seemed to be a country with a general 'feel good' factor. Americans had money, and they were spending it. England still had rationing, and, under a socialist government, the end of the 1940s was not terribly exciting.

Buddy wrote to tell me how lucky I was to be enjoying life in Florida, and thank me for the latest consignment of chocolate and other goodies that I had sent. Ernest was a wonderful correspondent, letting me know how well Paul was doing at Pinewood and how much he was looking forward to us all being together again. I swam in the sea, or in the Bath & Tennis Club pool, every day, and the skies were blue and the sun shone. It was perfect, but I found myself longing for the odd cloud or two, and, increasingly, I wanted to move on, to do something else and see other places, particularly New York, before the time came for me to go back to England.

I knew that it might be difficult to resign, but I had paid my own fare, to make it possible to move on without too many recriminations, and the relationship with Dale and Heather had been completely successful. They no longer refused to eat properly and wanted to gain the A+ that clean plates brought. I liked them both and we had had great fun together, but they should soon be going to school and my work would be over. I had been with Mr and Mrs McNulty for over five months, and I looked for the right moment to call it a day and resign. As is often the case, things happened to make me feel that that moment had come.

On one of my days off in February, Heather was not at all well. She had a cold and a slight temperature, but Mrs M was pleased to look after her little daughter, and there wasn't any reason to stop me leaving for a planned visit to West Palm Beach. I was about to go when Heather started to cry. "I want Jay! I don't want Mummy, I want Jay!" I was really upset for her mother, whom I liked, and I knew how she must feel. I told Heather, quite briskly, not to be so silly, but to be a good little girl and have a lovely day. On that, I quickly left the house. I suppose what had happened was inevitable, I had spent every day with Heather, and we had had lots of fun together, while her mother did the social things that a husband and a lot of money demanded. It was definitely time I moved on.

Had I been in any doubt, a second reason to leave emerged a few days later. At the Bath and Tennis club, where we had spent nearly every day, the children and I had enjoyed the full benefits of family membership. After lunch I always signed the bill, and to all intents and purposes, I had membership privileges. Obviously, though, there were several others there with their charges, and the club brought in a new rule. All 'staff' must wear a uniform, that would identify the role they were playing, and it must be clear that they were at the club as employees. It was the last straw and I started to plan the end of my life as a 'governess' and the start of an exciting new era in New York City.

It was slightly difficult to see just how this metamorphosis could be accomplished. I had virtually no money, and no one I could rely on to help me. No friends and no contacts, no specific skills and absolutely no idea what might or might not be possible. What I did have was complete confidence that, somehow or other, everything would turn out all right. The Palm Beach local newspaper gave me the first clue. There was an advertisement in the Personal Column, asking if anyone would be interested in sharing the cost of a car journey to Washington at the beginning of March, giving a telephone number to call.

I rang and spoke to a man called David, who had a strong southern accent. His home was in Georgia, and he worked as a civil servant in Washington.The journey from Florida would take about two days, as he wanted to visit his mother in Georgia, en route, and he had already found one of the two passengers he was looking for, a girl who would be getting off in Virginia. It sounded the perfect answer to my transport needs, an inexpensive trip to the capital and good company on the way. I promptly accepted the offer, and Dave said that he would be ready to leave Florida in the first week of March.

The next thing was to resign my job, which I suspected might not be a pleasant experience. Mr M had enjoyed the social cachet of having 'an English governess' for his children, and I hoped that he recognised my appointment had been both inexpensive and successful. I liked his wife immensely, and was always, (silently), on her side, when he put her down in public, which he frequently did. She let me try on her mink coat, which was wonderfully soft and warm, and quite unlike any of the other furs, like rabbit, that I had ever worn. The oil money was hers, but Mr M always behaved as though the affluent life style was due to his efforts. She once said, "I envy you, Jay!" which seemed totally ridiculous, but, of course, she thought I was free to do just what I liked.

Fortunately, Mr M was visiting at the weekend, so, after the children had gone to bed, I asked if I could speak to him on an urgent matter. I explained that, as I wanted to travel a little, before I went back to England at the end of the summer, it would be a great help if I could leave at the beginning of March. Both children would be starting school when they went back to New York at Easter, so I was sure my resignation would not unduly inconvenience anyone. He listened in stony silence, and when I asked if he could let me have a written reference, to prove my integrity to any future employer, he nodded coldly and left the room.

I never saw him again, as, that night, he flew back to New York. He left a brief testimonial that said I had been 'honest, sober and industrious'. It was about as insulting as he thought he could get away with, and his wife was quite upset when, angrily, I showed it to her. She apologised profusely, (I imagine she was not surprised at his rudeness), and offered to write something for me. She got a piece of headed paper and asked what I wanted her to say, so I dictated a fairly glowing report on my work and my character, which, incidentally, I never used.

It would be much harder to say goodbye to Dale and Heather, for I had grown very fond of them and we had had great fun together. The lessons seemed to have been successful, and Heather could read well, though my lack of arithmetical skills had, I was fairly sure, limited their progress in maths. Best of all, they were no longer quite so attention-seeking, and certainly much nicer to be with for any length of time. I had managed to save about two hundred dollars, or fifty pounds, from my salary and Christmas presents, so I was ready to set out on the next big adventure; footloose and fancy free!

Chapter 15

By the time Dave's car drew up outside the front door in Palm Beach the following week, I was really excited about what the future might hold. Mrs M and the two children gave me a cheerful send off, and I knew that it was very unlikely that I would ever see them again. The other passenger, for the journey up the East Coast on Route 1, was Eileen, a very pleasant thirty year old, who came from Richmond, Virginia, which she said was a beautiful city that had strong historical links with Great Britain.

We took it in turns to sit in the front of the car, to keep Dave company, and we both thought that he was a nice man, but rather heavy-going. However, he was a very good driver, so we had reached Savannah where his mother lived, by late afternoon. We stopped there for the night, booking two rooms in a local roadside motel, one for Dave and one for Eileen and me. I had never stayed in a motel before, as they simply didn't exist in England, so I was immensely impressed. Ours was a big room, with two huge beds and a large bathroom, with a bath as well as a shower. Moreover, it was not at all expensive, which was very good news on my extremely tight budget.

Dave went off to visit his mother, but came back to join us for dinner in a nearby restaurant, where he said the food was excellent. I had no idea what to order, so I asked our waiter what the local speciality was. He thought for a moment and then suggested something called 'grits', but when I said I'd have a plate of grits, they all fell about laughing, and I discovered why they were so amused when my order arrived. 'Grits' were some kind of grain that had been boiled, and made virtually tasteless. The meal was much better when a steak and mushrooms were added, and with lots of "You-alls", (pronounced "Yawl"), they relived the fun of the grits joke. I couldn't imagine how dull their lives must be, if that had been the rib-tickler of the day.

We got off to a good start the next morning, and the road took us through some lovely hilly countryside, in Georgia and then in the woods of South Carolina. The car radio was playing, very appropriately, "Nothing could be finer/ Than to be in Carolina/ In the morning", the signature tune of the local station, and I whole-heartedly endorsed those sentiments. I felt totally carefree, and the world was my oyster, just as long as it didn't prove to be too expensive! Dave and I said goodbye to Eileen in Virginia, and by the evening we were in the outskirts of Washington DC.

I wanted to do some sight-seeing before I went on to New York, so I asked him if he knew where I could get an inexpensive room, for two nights. He immediately offered me a put-u-up in his little flat, but I was not at all certain exactly what the offer entailed, so I thanked him but politely refused. After Eileen had left, he had told me a great deal about his life in Washington, which had not been easy. He was, he said, an alcoholic, and had experienced several 'lost weekends'. Just a sip of anything intoxicating, could set him off on the downward spiral, that invariably ended in disaster, and a spell in hospital. I told him that I was glad that he could be so honest, and he said that it had taken him a long time to feel that he could openly admit to being an alcoholic, or that a problem existed. He explained that doing so, was vital to acceptance of the 'illness' that was ruining his life.

However, he was certainly in remission, and seemed keen to take me around in Washington, so that I didn't miss the many exciting sights. That sounded fine, and after he had dropped me off at small hotel in the centre, we arranged to meet the next morning. He seemed very lonely, which I supposed went with the drink problem, but he was enthusiastic about the capital city, and all that it had to offer, so I was sure he'd be a very good guide.

Punctually, at ten the next morning, Dave arrived in his car to start the tour, and it really was fascinating. I loved the Potomac River, with the flowering cherry trees just starting to blossom, and the grandeur of the Lincoln Memorial, with the huge, wonderfully life-like, seated figure. The sight of The White House, with its rolling lawns, and the domed Capitol, looked familiar after years of seeing them on the films, and we took a walk down a street that had a statue of Puck, with the inscription, "Lord, what fools these mortals be!". A very suitable epitaph for a city that made a living from politics.

At the end of the day, we drove into Maryland, to eat at a superb fish restaurant, and he suggested that I should try their speciality, the 'Seafood Platter'. It was absolutely scrumptious, especially a delicious scallop-like piece, which was particularly sweet and moist. I asked what this was, so that I could have it again in the future, and they gave it a technical name. Later, back in England, I asked a fishmonger if I could order some, and there was no problem, except that I was then given the more popular name, 'cods' eyes'. I'm sorry to say that that was the end of my desire to ever eat it again.

The next morning I was due to take the Greyhound Bus, all the way to New York City, and Dave insisted on picking me up and driving me to the bus station. He had been very kind, and made me promise that, if I had any problems, I would come back to Washington, where he would help me to find a job. I should remember, he said, that the offer of a bed still stood. I had absolutely no intention of accepting such a dangerous option, but at least it was a possible fall-back if the worst happened. I thanked him again, shook his hand, and promised to keep in touch and let him know what happened. He waved the bus off and I never expected to see him again. I was wrong

The journey to New York seemed very long, and it was evening before the bus pulled into the terminus. Over the phone, I had booked a room for two nights in 'The Martha Washington Hotel for Women' which was near the centre, and it felt wonderful to be back in the buzz of the city that I had last seen, the previous October, when I disembarked from the Queen Elizabeth. I could only afford two nights at the hotel, so I urgently needed two things, somewhere to live and a job. It couldn't be that hard to find work, but I really didn't want to be resident, and I didn't want to look after children. The next morning, I got up bright and early and bought a paper that I had been told would have advertisements that might help.

As I scanned the 'Situations Vacant' column, the enormity of the task began to dawn on me. I had one more night at the hotel, and then I would only have enough money left to take the bus back to Washington, and enlist Dave's help, with all that that implied. I knew no-one else in the entire country, so there would be no other option. There were plenty of advertisements for domestic helps, and cooks and housekeepers, and no shortage of ones for shorthand typists and accountants, but I had none of the required skills. I didn't really know what I was looking for, but whatever it was, it wasn't there!

Then I spotted something quite different, in the 'Personal Column', offering, "A comfortable room and breakfast orange juice, in return for occasional baby-sitting. Call for interview.", and there was a telephone number. I was in the foyer of 'The Martha Washington Hotel', and I could see that there was a call box in one corner, so, checking that I had the right amount of change, I joined the queue to use the phone. It was a Manhattan number, and it just could be the answer to all my prayers. A comfortable room, was exactly what I wanted, and I had to have it by the following morning. It was a fairly tight deadline!

I am unlucky in queues. I always seem to be behind people who take ages to do whatever it is they're doing. At a railway station ticket office, when I want to buy a simple return, the person in front of me usually seems to be booking a world tour for a large group, and in a traffic queue, if I change lanes, the lane I have just left, speeds forward and passes me. Waiting for the phone behind a woman who chatted at length to a friend, and then made at least two other calls, was agonising but I did, finally, get my turn. I dialled the number, but got the engaged signal, so I feared that a steady stream of applicants were making appointments for interviews. Because there were several others waiting for the phone, I redialled the number, and to my relief, this time I heard the ringing tone at the other end.

A woman's voice answered, and I said that I had seen the advertisement for a baby-sitter in the paper and I would very much like to come for an interview. She paused briefly and then asked if I could manage four o'clock ? I assured her that I could, and gave her my name. She told me the address on East 84th Street, and said she would see me at four. I was certainly going to have to walk there, as taxis were out of the question on my limited budget, so I set out very early to take a look at that part of the city, between Lexington and 3rd Avenues.

When I found East 84th Street, it was in a very smart area, only two or three blocks from Central Park and 5th Avenue. The house looked quite big, (I think they were called 'brownstone' houses), with a basement, and steps up to the front door. On the stroke of four I rang the bell and a very pleasant woman, in her mid-thirties came to let me in. She introduced herself as Mrs Jessop, and explained what the 'job' actually was.

She and her husband, Jack, the editor of Fortune Magazine, had two little boys, Amos and Nathaniel. On occasions, they needed a baby-sitter, but it would always be in the evening, so that the person involved could work, full time, elsewhere. She was very anxious that I should understand that there was absolutely no salary, or payment of any kind. The room was in exchange for the baby-sitting. I really liked the idea, and said so, explaining that I had been looking after two children in Palm Beach, for the past five months, and I now I wanted to do something else After a quick tour of the house, which did look big and comfortable inside. I was shown the patio garden, which had a spectacular, full-sized fountain that cascaded into a huge round stone basin, and I knew I would love to live there.

I had hoped that I might be offered the job, but, of course, there had been a lot of applicants, and several others had still to be interviewed. Mrs Jessop said she would be able to give me the final answer, the following day. This definitely created a problem, as the bus for Washington left mid-morning, so I would need to have an answer by ten. I explained it all, and I thought she understood, but I walked back to the hotel, rather disappointed that the interview had not had a positive outcome. However,

I had given her the Martha Washington telephone number, and all I could do now was wait and hope.

I didn't sleep well that night. There were too many imponderables, and luck was going to play a major role in my future plans. I had done all I could, but that might not have been enough, so I packed my case and went down to the foyer, to hand-in the keys to my room. There were four receptionists on duty along the counter, rather like cashiers in a bank. I went to each in turn to explain that I was waiting for a very important telephone call, and would be sitting on the long bench just in front of them. Then I bought a paper and sat down to wait.

Nine o'clock came, then half past nine, and nothing happened. The hotel phones kept ringing, and I kept standing up and giving the receptionists questioning looks, but a headshake always told me that the call was not for me. At a quarter to ten, I went to each of them in turn, just to check they knew my name and where I was sitting. They certainly got the impression that I was fairly desperate, and muttered sympathetic nothings like, "Don't worry, we'll call you at once", and gave me reassuring smiles. At ten o'clock, I accepted, for the first time, that I really was going to have to catch that bus to Washington. I gave one final look at each of the girls on the counter, picked up my case, and walked slowly towards the revolving glass door that led out onto the street. I had my hand on the glass panel as a voice shouted, "Jay Norris! There's a call for you!" Just one more step and it would have been too late.

Mrs Jessop was very apologetic. She was sorry it was so late, but if I was still interested, they would very much like to offer me the post. She had been delayed by a friend, and was afraid she might have missed me. Well, she very nearly had! She told me to take a taxi and they would pay. I enthusiastically, accepted both offers, and ten minutes later I was in East 84th Street, walking up the steps to the front door of the house that was to be my very happy home, until I left America three months later.

Chapter 16

The 'comfortable room and breakfast orange juice' turned out well for both parties, especially me. The Jessops were a delightful family. Eunice was a poetess, and had published a version of Æsop's Fables in verse, that I thought was really original and beautifully presented. Her husband, Jack, in his early forties, was the editor of 'Fortune', the national business and financial magazine, a part of the prestigious Time/Life syndicate. He was an academic, handsome and sophisticated, and they made a charming couple. The two boys were four and six, adored each other and were quietly happy, which was very nice to see. In the whole three months that I lived with them, I never once heard an angry voice, which has to be a pretty remarkable record for any family.

My room was definitely comfortable, the breakfast orange juice delicious, and, when the Jessops realised that I had virtually no money, they gave me evening dinner as well. My first priority now was to find a source of income, and I was ready to try anything. I answered an advertisement for the door to door selling of goods made by the blind, and was given me several roads to cover, with a supply of samples, to show to prospective customers. It was very hard work, as it was 'cold calling', knock on the door and hope you may make a sale. It was 'commission only', no sale no pay, and I hardly earned enough to pay my bus fare to the area. It was, however, a useful experience, as I found that I enjoyed selling, and that, in the USA, my English accent was worth its weight in gold.

I started searching the newspaper columns for jobs as a saleswoman, and quite soon I saw one that seemed a possibility. The work would be related to women's wards in hospitals, and the firm was based in Long Island, which was easily accessible from Manhattan. My three years in the VAD would be a good recommendation, and I wondered what the 'product' could possibly be. My call, requesting an interview, answered that question. The phone response was, "This is General Diaper Service! Can I help you?" I had no idea what a diaper was, or what might be involved in the 'service', but it seemed I could pick up an application form, in office hours, on Monday 'thru' Friday, if I wanted to join the sales' team. The Jessops, when asked, said they had heard of the firm, and they were very amused that I didn't know that a diaper was a baby's nappy! It seemed that, in America, mothers needn't wash any nappies, and, better still, didn't even need to buy any. Firms existed which would provide the nappies, collect the dirty ones and leave a fresh supply three or more times a week. It seemed a great idea!

The headquarters of General Diaper Service was a big laundry complex, on an industrial site in Long Island. There was a door at the side of the building with the word 'Reception' boldly displayed, and I went in to collect the form. The receptionist suggested that I should sit down and fill it in there and then, and they would process the information immediately. She told me that interviews were being held that afternoon, and, if I cared to wait, I could be on the list. I jumped at the chance of an early start to my sales' career, and wondered what kind of questions they would fire at me. I was not expecting a set intelligence test, but that is exactly what I got.

It wasn't particularly difficult, and it was followed by a word association test, when an interviewer fired a word at you, and you had to respond with the first word that came into your mind. Tactfully, when the word was "Boss!" I replied, "Kind!" and I passed. Finally, I was seen by one of the executives, who explained what the job involved. Sales were made in maternity wards, to women who had just had their babies. Representatives would go into a ward and canvass bed to bed for customers. Orders could be taken, and brought back to HQ, the service would then start on an agreed date. No deposit was required, but the new customer had to sign 'the promise to pay' which, I supposed, was legally enforceable.

Some hospitals, he said, welcomed the presence of the sales force, as providing a service to the patients, but others were less keen, or were syndicated to a rival firm, and then admission was more difficult and might involve a degree of finesse. Did I feel I could cope with such problems? I replied that I certainly could, as I had done door to door selling for the blind, which was not an easy option. I then asked the sixty-four dollar question; what was the salary? If he had said commission only, I would have politely declined the job. If it was on a sales plus commission basis, I might be interested, though my preference would be for salary only, which was exactly what he did offer, plus the incentive of an extra bonus gift out of a catalogue.

Almost as an afterthought, he asked me the one question I was dreading, "Do you have a driving licence?" The truthful answer would have been 'No', but I remembered seeing that eight year old boy, in Oklahoma, who could drive his sister to school, so I replied, "Yes, but, of course, it's an English licence." "That's fine," he answered," but you must pass the New York State test, within seven days. All right?" I nodded, but it was very far from all right. I couldn't afford to take lessons, so I just hoped that driving a car was as easy as it looked. At this point my interviewer offered his hand, "Welcome to General Diaper Service, Jay. We are delighted to have a representative from England on the sales' team. Report here on Monday at 9 am, and we can register all your particulars in our records." I thanked him profusely for at last I had a job.

I hurried back to give the news to the Jessops and they were fascinated by the idea of selling anything in a Maternity Ward, so I promised I would give them a blow by blow description of the sales techniques,. I didn't mention the driving licence hurdle, in case they felt obliged to offer help, and I was sure I could overcome any difficulty myself. I arrived in Long Island promptly at 9 am on the following Monday, and after a brief visit to the office, I met the Sales Director, Joe, and another salesman, Al, who was to be my mentor. Joe wished me success, and gave, what turned out to be, his customary blessing, "Go with God, and come back with orders!" Al and I got into a white Chevrolet, with 'General Diaper Service' inscribed in big blue letters on both sides, and we drove off quickly to our first port of call, a maternity hospital in the New York borough of Queens.

Al was a very pleasant, slightly portly, Italian American, who was an extremely keen salesman, and was an excellent teacher of the best way to succeed with the new mothers we were about to meet. As we drove along he explained the procedure that I must follow when I was taking an order, and added a few little tips on what not to do, just in case I didn't figure it out for myself. He seemed very interested to have met a real, live Englishwoman, and warned me to speak slowly to potential customers, who might find my accent difficult to understand. I was only half listening, as my focus was mainly on everything he did as he drove the car, and how I was going to talk him into letting me have a go.

When we arrived at the hospital, we parked on the street and walked into the reception area. The Maternity Ward was clearly signposted, so we followed the corridor down to the Sister's Room. She was writing a report, but looked up as we stood by the door. She obviously recognised Al and said at once, "Ah, General Diaper Service? You can go on in!" and went back to what she was doing, Al thanked her, and we went into quite a large ward, with about ten beds in it, each with a little cot beside it. It was a delightful sight, all the young mothers and their new babies, some just a day or so old.

We went over to the nearest bed, in which lay a smiling pretty girl. Very professionally, and with considerable charm, Al began his sales pitch, "Good morning, madam. I am from General Diaper Service. Would you like me to arrange diaper service for you when you return home?" Her smile widened. "That sounds a great idea!" Al explained exactly how the service worked, and within five minutes we were moving to the next bed with the signed order in our hands. Money for jam!

As though to demonstrate how hard a sell it might be sometimes, the next mother turned him down with a brief, "No thanks!", and, promptly, with a friendly smile, Al accepted the refusal, and we moved on. The third woman needed a little persuasion, suggesting she would like to give the idea some thought, but Al pointed out the advantages of having the service up and running as soon as she went home, and she eventually signed up. It took just under an hour to approach all ten patients, and we left with six orders, three refusals and a maybe, which Al said was a very good result.

Back outside in the car, he explained the selling method he used. There were, he said, three basic types of potential customer, whatever you were selling. The first would be those who wanted the 'item', and who immediately said yes. The second group were always going to say no, their minds already made up, and they wouldn't buy if you spent all day. It was the third group that tested your skill, for they had not decided either way, and needed to be persuaded, so they were the ones who took the salesman's time. We had seen all three kinds in the ward, and he felt pleased with the number of firm orders we had been given. It was a very good lesson, and I felt that, once I had mastered the 'spiel', I would be able to sell diaper service reasonably successfully. My next challenge was to sell Al on the idea of teaching me how to pass the driving test within the next seven days.

I took the direct approach. "I like the car, Al. It's a Chevy, isn't it? May I try it?" He, at once, agreed, got out of the driver's seat and came round to my side. "OK, Jay, move over, it's all yours!" I shuffled across into the driver's seat, and took hold of the steering wheel. (So far, so good!) I put a hand on the gear shift, as I had seen him do. It was on the side of the steering wheel, and easily watched as we had driven along. I shuffled my feet over the pedals and let out a very dramatic gasp, "Oh, Al, it's all different from my car in England! Everything's on the wrong side! It'll be like learning all over again!"

The amazing luck was, that he believed me, and actually thought that English cars were totally different. I started up the engine, with the foot starter, as he had, and pushed the gear lever upwards, we juddered and the engine cut out. I tried again taking my foot off one of the pedals, and the same thing happened. Al was anxious to help and so he told me what to do. "Switch on, depress the clutch pedal, get into gear, gently rev. Then slowly take your foot off the clutch, and press the accelerator, with the other foot!" I did as he said, and it worked for we slid forward.

It wasn't that difficult! His agonised shout of "Brake!", told me we were about to career down the road, but I was delighted with the start I had made, in acquiring this vital new skill.

When we got back to Long Island, Joe was pleased with the number of orders we had taken, and Al and I got several of the points, that would finally translate into gifts from the catalogue. He sprang the news on me that he had booked my driving test for Friday, four days away, and Al and I could have the morning off to go to the centre and use the firm's car for the test. I tried to look pleased, but I knew there were skills like reversing and parking, that I had to master in the next three days, to have any hope of passing.

During the next three days I took every chance to practise my driving skills, between our visits to various maternity units in Brooklyn, the Bronx, and Manhattan. The most difficult manoeuvre, as far as I was concerned, was the three point parking between two other cars. You had to go past the first car, until you were level with it, reverse into the space, and then make just one forward and one reverse adjustment to land up parked close to the line of the kerb, equidistant from the other two cars. I found it virtually impossible, but it was a must-do for passing the test. Al was really kind and he never even hinted that he doubted my story of having an English licence. Perhaps he just thought that over there we were pretty poor drivers!

Friday came all too quickly, and I met Al at the driving centre in Long Island, half an hour before the time of my test. We had a little drive round the block and I had one last go at parking in the space between two cars, but nothing had changed, I couldn't do it. Back at the centre, Al wished me luck, so I waited in the car for my examiner and almost immediately he arrived. He was quite young and seemed very cheerful, for one with such a life-threatening job as going with learner drivers into the aggressive traffic of the New York City streets.

We set off without any problem, and, one by one, I did the various stops and starts, and twists and turns, that the format of the test required. Our final stop took us to a quiet area, with a row of shops, and a line of cars parked in front of them. There was a space between two of them and it would be reasonably tight to get in to. Then that surge of adrenalin, the excitement of the moment, that had given me unearned success in countless exams, took over, and when he pointed to the space and told me to park in it, I did it perfectly. He was suitably impressed, and muttered "Well done, that's great!" and told me to drive back to the centre. Al was waiting anxiously, but when he saw the examiner shake my hand and smile, he guessed that all was well. We stopped for a congratulatory drink on the way back to our HQ, and Al showed me pictures of the wife and the three little daughters he obviously adored. I owed my success to his efforts, and he was delighted when I told him so.

Joe was waiting for us, and told me that, now I had a New York State driving licence I would be working on my own. I should see the transport department to get a car allocated to me, so that everything would be ready for the following Monday morning. He also passed on the news that another young lady was joining the sales force, and that her name was Mary.

Chapter 17

When I gave the Jessops the good news that I had passed the driving test, which meant I could keep the job at General Diaper Service, they were really pleased. We all got on so well together that it would have been a shame if I had had to look for a residential post somewhere else. They asked if I had made any friends in New York, and I had to admit it had all been too frenetic, so far. However, I told them that, coming over on the QE from England, I had enjoyed the company of one of the ship's officers, and had promised to get in touch with him, if I ever came back to New York. They immediately said that I must keep my promise and I should contact the Cunard Office, to see if a telephone number could be passed on to my friend. I agreed to do just that, though I wasn't at all sure that Dickie wouldn't have transferred his affection elsewhere. Five months seemed a long time for him to stay interested in someone he had only known for about a week!.

However, to my surprise, the next time the ship docked on the East River, I got an urgent call, asking me to meet him for dinner that evening, so that we could get re-acquainted. He suggested a very good restaurant called 'The Russian Bear', as a meeting place, and by eight o'clock we were laughing and talking together as if we had never been apart. I told him all about Oklahoma and Florida, and he spoke about life on the ship, but we were really concerned with the present, and planned to meet whenever he came to New York. It was clearly going to be great fun for us both. Little did I realise it, but another very important friendship was just about to start.

I met Mary, the new member of the sales' team, when I got back from my first day as a solo operator. I was very tired because the driving had been quite traumatic. It is one thing to have a piece of paper that says you're a qualified driver, and quite another to be driving on busy roads, when you really don't know what you're doing. The sales' promotion in the hospitals was comparatively easy. It was getting from A to B in the car that was difficult! Mary was sitting talking to Joe when I came into the office. He introduced us and then immediately rushed off to deal with a problem in the diaper collection department.

She was in her very early twenties, of medium build with a lively, attractive face, short brown curly hair, and horn-rimmed glasses, I liked the intensity of her expression as she listened to the sad tale of my struggle in the city traffic, and I made her laugh with the story of my adventures on the motorway. The firm's cars were roughly the same colour and shape as the ones driven by the police, and going rather slowly on a main route, I had gathered a queue of about twenty vehicles behind me, as no one liked to pass a police car. Finally, someone took the risk and then saw the General Diaper Service logo, so sped off, followed by a line of disgruntled motorists, who had hooted their annoyance as they passed.

Mary was from West Virginia, where her father was a GP. She was studying medicine and wanted to specialise in paediatrics when she qualified. She had taken the sales job in Long Island to earn some vacation money, and I was able to tell her that it seemed to be a jolly good firm to work for. She had been extremely amused to be given an intelligence test to make sure she was clever enough to sell diaper service, and, like me, she thought that 'the word association test' was a total waste of time. We agreed that you would have to be pretty dense to follow the word "Boss", with anything other than a compliment. I wanted to know if she had a New York State driving licence, and she said that hers was from West Virginia, but she had been driving for several years, so getting re-tested didn't present a problem.

When I asked whether she had any friends in the city, she blushed slightly and told me about Bob, whose father lectured in science at

Columbia University. They were living together, to see how well they got on and Bob had a holiday job selling perfume to retail outlets, so their bed-sitter tended to be rather heavy with the smell of cheap scent. I really liked Mary. She was bright and fun to talk to, so I hoped we might see something of each other outside work. I enjoyed her stories about Bob, and hoped that I would meet him before long.

Meanwhile, the selling of diaper service kept us busy. It was not always as simple as it had first seemed, in that the General reps could only go, openly, into institutions where official permission had been given. In such places, where I imagined that a premium of some kind was paid, we were supposed to have sole rights to make sales. We could arrive, as I did with Al on my first day, go from bed to bed, and then leave. It was all above board, but there were other scenarios that were explained to us later, known as 'Operation Sneak' and they were definitely secret and extremely dramatic.

Several other diaper service companies existed, but our main competitor was 'Stork', and they, too, had hospitals, where only their reps were allowed to canvass the patients. To gain access to this market, we had to resort to subterfuge, and the perceived method was to buy a bunch of flowers, and pretend to be a visitor. If you were questioned about who you had come to see, you had to make up an appropriate name, which could be Mrs Cohen, in a Jewish area, or Mrs O'Brien, in a predominantly Irish district, and so on. Having got into the ward, the flowers would provide a cover story if you were caught, otherwise you would take orders for diaper service, as unobtrusively as possible, and quickly leave. Mary hated 'Operation Sneak', but I quite enjoyed the role play, and the excitement of the risk of being unmasked as an 'enemy agent'.

The managers at General Diaper Service took the search for new customers very seriously, hardly surprisingly, for it was their bread and butter, but as temporary employees, Mary and I could only wonder at the lengths they were prepared to go to, to get good results. They would have endless discussions at sales' staff meetings, on how and when new efforts to increase productivity could be tried. There was something quite bizarre in watching grown men heatedly disagreeing on the revision of methods for the delivery and collection of babies' nappies. An in-house magazine for customers, called 'Baby Talk', had advice on the latest things to buy for Baby, and discussions of modern methods of rearing a happy and healthy offspring. The firm was making very good profits as there was a growing market for diaper service. The end of the war, and the return of the GIs, had brought with it the inevitable baby boom.

My social life had improved by leaps and bounds since Mary and I had become friends. Bob turned out to be a real charmer; very engaging, handsome and intelligent, and one of the best tellers of jokes I had ever met. He was Jewish, but an agnostic, and we had fascinating discussions about religion and the existence of God. Mary had once been a devout Catholic and she pointed out that, if I really believed in the presence of Jesus at the mass, I would be there every day. Since my attendance at church was a rather irregular Sunday event, she had a point.

Bob was part of a group of bright, young New Yorkers, who were determined to enjoy life to the full, and swapped partners at the drop of a hat. Very naively, they seemed genuinely surprised when things didn't turn out the way they expected. Ed, who was Polish, was a good example of the muddle that some of these new friends had made of their lives. He had married Gina, a very sweet girl, but he felt that she lacked sexual experience, so he asked his friends, one after another, to sleep with her. They obliged without hesitation but during the experiment, she, not surprisingly, met someone she liked better than Ed, so she left him.

When we first met, at an all-night poetry-reading session, Ed was trying to bolster his damaged ego by propositioning any available female talent he encountered, so quite seriously, he asked me, out of the blue, when could we go to bed together? It was not an approach likely to succeed and I turned down the invitation, for it was certainly a very different world from anything I had experienced before. Bob told me later, that Ed had been quite upset at being refused and wondered what was wrong with him that women did not seem keen to accept his offers.

I think someone once said that England and America were two nations separated by a common language, and there were times when this was all too clear. I had no intention of picking up an American accent, but words like 'pavement' and 'petrol' had to be changed to 'sidewalk' and 'gas', if anyone was to understand what I was talking about. I had problems, initially, when I ordered coffee and biscuits. The man in the café asked, "How many biscuits do you want?", and raised his eyebrows when I told him that two would be enough. The arrival of a cup of coffee and two huge scones, explained why he had been surprised.

The stress on syllables could make a huge difference to comprehension. In my sales' chat to customers I had to mention that all the diapers were 'laboratory' tested. My normal pronunciation had to be changed to '*labre-*tree' or no one would have known what I was talking about. Even the long and short 'a' could cause a problem, as I found when I ordered tomato soup, and they asked "What?", so I tried 'termayter', and I got some!

In England, an accent would generally show how well the speaker had been educated, but in the States, it usually showed where they came from. There were, however, some non-u pronunciations, and they were quite the opposite. The word 'ate', was 'et' in England, but this was definitely not acceptable in up-market New York, where it had to be 'ayte'. I was interested to discover that egalitarian America, had its own snob culture, and there was even an exclusive group of women, calling themselves 'Daughters of the Revolution', who boasted that their ancestors had come over in The Mayflower.

It was somewhat surprising to learn, by a chance remark, that Bob did not have a driving licence, and, as I had been a driver for all of six weeks, I confidently offered to give him lessons. I had started to enjoy the excitement of beetling along in a car, and the wonderful freedom it gave. No longer did I have to wait for over-crowded buses, or, worse still, walk, to get where I was going. Buddy had hated walking, which she thought was a terrible waste of time, and we had always cycled everywhere, whatever the weather. I thought a car was much better. You were warm and dry, you didn't have to pedal, and you got to your destination very quickly.

I only hated driving once, in New York, when my engine cut out in the middle of Times Square. Cars hooted, policemen blew whistles, and though I pressed the foot starter so hard that it went through the sole of my shoe, nothing happened. There was traffic chaos, and I was the cause. I seriously considered getting out and walking away, but at that exact moment, the engine responded to the desperate pressing of my shoe, and I quickly drove away, to the hisses of 'Woman driver!' from my fellow road users.

The plan to teach Bob meant that I would keep the General Diaper Service car overnight, and we could go, with Mary, to Coney Island, where there would be less traffic on the roads. She loved the idea, as it was vital that he learnt to drive but she certainly did not want to risk the break-up of their relationship, by trying to teach him, She had also been traumatised by failing her New York State driving test at the first attempt, despite several years on the roads of West Virginia. It was early June, and the weather was comfortably warm, so we could have a swim off the beautiful sandy beach, when the lesson was over.

The idea worked well, as I always managed to 'borrow' the car, taking care to fill it up before I returned it the following day, and Bob was a quick learner. We did have one little blip, when he was practising backing, and reversed into a parked car, but it was only a little bump, so we drove away fairly quickly! Coney Island was a fun place to visit, with switchback rides and lively roundabouts. The sea was always calm, though there were notices that warned swimmers of potential danger from strong currents. They were happy, carefree days, and I wrote to tell Ernest and Buddy all about Bob and Mary, who hoped to come to England on a research bursary, once they had qualified. They knew all about Paul, and why I was having a year away from home, and they understood what a devastating effect a long absence could have on a relationship.

Bob had spent the end of the war in the American merchant navy, as a medical officer, on ships carrying livestock in coastal waters. He was only a student, in his late teens, but he was responsible for the health of the crew, which included making sure they were 'protected', when they visited brothels ashore. He told us that he had had to buy the protection, known as 'rubbers', from a local drug store, and it created some surprise when he asked for five hundred. The sales' clerk thought she had misheard the number. "Did you say five HUNDRED, sir?" "Yes," Bob replied, "I'm going away for a long weekend!" His stories of the crew and their relationships with the sheep they carried, were also very funny, but, I'm afraid, completely unrepeatable.

The work had also had a very serious side, for Bob's only medical knowledge came from a book, supplied by the merchant navy. Therefore, when a member of the crew suffered a strangulated hernia, that had to be operated on, Bob, aged only seventeen, had to perform the operation, following instructions given over the ship's radio. He said he was shaking like a leaf when the operation was over, and was very relieved when the patient not only survived, but recovered completely.

Of course I introduced Bob and Mary to Dickie, and they really liked him. Every time the QE came to New York, he would phone and we would go out to the countryside around the city, to give him a break from 'life on the ocean wave'. I was a little worried that he still seemed to drink rather a lot of neat gin, though, in fairness, he never seemed to be other than relaxed and happy. Quite what was happening to his liver, I had no idea, but he was a grown man and I presumed that he knew what he was doing, so I didn't interfere. It was helpful for him that I only liked the odd glass of wine, and drinking binges were certainly not something I enjoyed.

I had, however, developed a bad habit of my own, as I had started to smoke. Buddy often lit a cigarette, as many nurses did, and I smoked socially, when I wanted to join in with the rest of the group. I had, however, never inhaled, and I was a 'take it or leave it' smoker. Watching me puff on a cigarette, Bob noticed that I didn't inhale, and pointed out that I was missing the whole point of smoking, the pleasant effect of the nicotine that the tobacco contained. I was wasting my money, if I only puffed out the smoke. Wasting my money? What a dreadful thought. So I worked hard to learn how to inhale. It wasn't easy, and it made me feel rather groggy, but I persevered, and within two months I could do it, and I was hooked on nicotine!

Chapter 18

The summer of 1948, in New York City, was certainly very hot, and in July, for the first time in my life, I had beads of sweat on my forehead. The humidity affected everything and everyone, and the energy of the city seemed to fade as the temperature rose. I knew that I would be going back to England in August, in time for Paul's fifth birthday on 28th, so I booked a passage on the QE to arrive in Southampton by August 26th. Ernest and Buddy were already making plans for the grand reunion celebrations in England, and the Jessops had made it clear that, the day before I left, they would hold a goodbye party for me in New York.

There were several loose ends that needed to be tied up, and the first was when to resign my job with General Diaper Service. On the whole, I had enjoyed sales promotion, except for the doubtful ethics of the hard sell. It was certainly possible that we often put sales pressure on vulnerable women, who could not afford diaper service, even though they would like to have it. I tried to dissuade some potential customers from signing up, by reminding them how many dollars it was going to cost. However, they often seemed to think I was trying to deprive them of their human rights, and were not pleased with my efforts to keep them solvent!

The question of when to leave General Diaper Service was settled, once and for all, by a very distressing incident. I was on 'Operation Sneak' in one of a rival's maternity units, when I went into a private room at the bottom of the ward corridor. There were two people there, a woman, in bed, with her head in her hands, and a well-dressed man, sitting silently in a chair. There was none of the joy, that is so much a part of maternity units, and my immediate feeling was that I had walked in on a row between the woman and her husband. Nothing daunted, I asked if I could arrange diaper service for them. To my horror the woman started to cry and the man leapt from his chair as if he was going to attack me. "Get out!" he shouted, "Get out!", and then I saw that the cot beside the bed was empty, and realised that the baby must have died.

I rushed out to the car and drove back to Long Island to see Joe. I was really upset as I knew that, if it had been one of our hospitals, the ward sister would have warned me not to go into the room. I told him exactly what had happened, and how potentially dangerous I thought 'Sneak' was. He looked concerned, and I waited for him to say how sorry he was. In fact, what he did say genuinely shocked me. "Did you mention General Diaper Service?" Angrily, I told him that I hadn't, but that hardly mattered. "Well, such things happen," he said. "Thank goodness they didn't know who you were."

I then realised the truth. He was a nice man, who wouldn't have hurt a fly, but business was business, and so long as no damage was done, he really couldn't see why I was making such a fuss. I handed in my resignation the next morning.

In Washington, in March, I had promised Dave that I would let him know how things turned out in New York, and I felt slightly guilty that I had not been in touch since he waved me off at the bus station. I wrote him a quick note to say that my stay in America was almost over, as I was leaving on the QE in the second week of August. I said that I had had a wonderful time, thanked him for his help, adding that, if he ever came to England, he should let me know. I never expected to see him again, but, once again, I was wrong!

Already there were plans for what was going to happen in England, after my year away. Strix, the head of Pinewood, where Ernest and Paul had been staying, offered to give me a teaching post at the school, when I got back home. It sounded like a very good idea, as it would solve the problem of where we were going to live. Buddy knew that we would not be going back to Enfield, but she had got quite used to taking the bus to Great Amwell to visit the school, so when I accepted a temporary appointment there, she was quite pleased. Ernest had already booked a 'second honeymoon' week, at a hotel in Broadstairs, on the Kent coast, and it really did seem that my year's absence had solved many of our problems. I hoped so, from the bottom of my heart, for everyone's sake.

My last week in New York was very exciting. An article about my job with General Diaper Service, that Jack Jessop had asked me to write for 'Fortune Magazine', was going to be published in the September issue. It had a new title, "The Adventures of a Diaper Salesman', and a company had bought the film rights. When I sold the story, I had agreed to forfeit any profit from future deals, but it was still mind-boggling to hear that Lucille Ball was being considered to play me. Later, I learnt that the producer had died, and so the project was abandoned, but I was nearly famous !

On my last day in New York, the QE was not arriving until the afternoon, so I knew that Dickie would be a little late for the goodbye party at East 84th Street. All my new friends would be there, especially Bob and Mary, who were coming on board the next morning to have a final drink, before the ship sailed. My luggage was ready and everything was packed, for I was going home.

The party had really got going by the time Dickie appeared, and he looked a little the worse for wear, but very happy. There was delicious food and lots of Californian champagne, supplied by the Jessops, and gloriously warm weather, so we all gathered around the fountain in the courtyard and swapped memories of my past five months in New York. Dickie had said that he had to get back to the ship by midnight, so at about a quarter to twelve, I got the car started and he was helped into the passenger seat. He was a little unsteady but I was going to take him right up to the QE gangway, so all should be well.

On the way to the East River he fell asleep, I just thought he was tired after a long day, but when we arrived at the dock, and I tried to wake him, I realised he was dead drunk. It wasn't immediately obvious what I should do. I certainly couldn't carry him on board, and the whole area was totally deserted, except for a few cabs by the dockside. I tried to wake him by gently hitting him, but that just made him flail about, trying to hit me back. There was nothing for it but to drive back to East 84th Street, and get some help from the partygoers, if they were still sober.

As I turned the car to start back, it ran out of petrol. What a scenario! A woman, in a parked car, with a drunken sailor, in a red light district by the docks. I left Dickie snoring and went over to a taxi, to ask the driver where I might find a garage to get some 'gas'. He pointed to one, not too far away, so I walked there and they produced a can, which they filled with petrol. Back at the car, Dickie was still asleep, but I put in the petrol and drove back to the garage to return the can. It was not the best ending to my last day in America.

Once I got to the party, the men took over, Dickie was carried into the house, sobered up with innumerable cups of coffee, and somebody-else drove him back to the ship. When I saw him on board the next day, he was very apologetic, but also a little upset as, while I was off getting the petrol, someone had opened the car door and stolen his wallet. I didn't say "It served you right!", but it did.

The next morning, when Bob and Mary had driven me to the ship and had come on board for a final glass of champagne, I was amazed to see Dave from Washington, coming towards us. He had found out when the Q E was sailing, and had driven the three hundred miles from Washington, just to say goodbye. I introduced him to the others, and we all chatted about our various experiences, when the "All ashore!" announcement came over the loudspeakers. I gave Bob and Mary big hugs and looked forward to seeing them in England, and went to shake Dave's hand, but he had other ideas. I got enthusiastically kissed, which came as a big surprise, as I hadn't realised we were quite so friendly, but it didn't worry me unduly, as it seemed unlikely that I would ever see him again. As usual, I was wrong!

The voyage back on the QE was absolutely splendid. Dickie had told me to put my stuff into the cabin named on my ticket, but not to unpack, as he thought he could get it swapped for something better. He certainly did. I was given a swish double cabin, with a porthole, which was the height of luxury. We had six enjoyable days before we reached

Southampton, and I realised what a huge advantage it was to have a friend on the staff. He said that he hoped we might meet in England sometime, when he was on leave, but I secretly thought that was unlikely, which was quite sad.

As the train steamed into Waterloo Station, Ernest, Buddy and Paul, were waiting on the platform, and it was wonderful to see them. Paul had grown quite tall for a little boy of almost five, and didn't seem to have forgotten me, which was a great relief. Everyone was delighted that the parting was over, and there seemed to be a new understanding of how we could all be happy together. Back in Enfield, we talked through the plans for the immediate future.

There would be a birthday party for Paul, on 28th, and then Ernest and I were off on the train to Broadstairs, on the Kent coast, to have a week together, before we went to Pinewood, and I started my teaching there. Apparently, Strix had agreed to let us have the stable block, as our very first home. There were two rooms, plus a bathroom and a kitchen and Ernest had promised that we would repaint it all, which sounded great fun. Paul would stay in the school, as a boarder, but, of course, he would come to see us whenever he liked. This certainly looked like the new beginning we had all hoped for.

The birthday party, two days later, was a great success. There were several other little boys, and they kicked balls around in the garden, chased each other all over the house in an energetic game of hide and seek and vigorously tucked into all the food that Buddy had carefully prepared, or, more probably, bought from Sainsbury's! I had brought a Red Indian outfit from New York, and Ernest and Buddy gave him his first two-wheeled bicycle. There was just one small problem; he fell off every time he tried to ride it. Paul was a very happy, if slightly bruised, little boy by the time I tucked him in and gave him an especially big birthday kiss.

Ernest and I went to King's Cross the next day, and then to Charing Cross for the train to Broadstairs. Apparently, the hotel we were going to, had once belonged to Charles Dickens, and he had written 'David

Copperfield' there. At least, that's what they claimed. It was right up at the top of a hill, and we walked down into the centre to have a drink to celebrate our reunion. Incredibly, we were at ease with each other. It was as though I'd just come back from a long holiday, and I told Ernest all about Bob and Mary, and hoped that, one day, he would meet them.

It was a help that, while I was away, we had exchanged long letters, so he knew all about Oklahoma and Florida, and the Jessops in New York. For his part, Ernest told me about Pinewood, the stable building that was to be our home, and the friends he'd made on the staff, who sounded quite a jolly group. Neither of us asked too many questions. I remembered Buddy's warning that a handsome man, on his own, might find another interest, but I never asked Ernest if he did, and he never asked me. Neither of us believed in 'kiss and tell', for whatever had or had not happened wasn't important. What did matter was that we made a success of our marriage from now on, and we could certainly make a good start by having a relaxed 'second honeymoon' in Broadstairs.

I had only been there once before when I was a little girl. Then I was playing on the crowded beach, when someone threw a stone from the top of the cliffs and, though there were hundreds of people there, it hit me! I still had a scar to prove it, but this was a much happier visit. Broadstairs was a little seaside town, with high white cliffs, a long beach and a big harbour, which was very popular in Victorian times, hence the Dickensian connection. The little winding streets going down to the sea were not meant for motor cars, and there are now lots of bistro style cafes. It is still slightly 'old–fashioned', and at the annual Dickens festival, the residents help that illusion by dressing in Victorian costume.

The weather was warm and sunny and, through our daily excursions to the shops, the beach and the museums, we soon knew the pretty little town quite well. The best thing was that we got to know each other, all over again, and it seemed that, this time, we were both determined to make our marriage a success. All too soon, however, our week ended and we made the journey back to Enfield to pick up Paul, and go on to Pinewood. Buddy, who had vigorously opposed my trip to the USA, made us laugh by telling everyone what a wonderful idea it had been, and how much she loved hearing all about life in America. We took a taxi to Great Amwell and I told Ernest that, now I could drive, I would take the test and we could buy our very own car. He loved the idea.

Chapter 19

As we came up the drive at Pinewood, I remembered how much it had impressed me on my first visit. The elegant old house, the spreading cedar branches above the green lawn, and the general air of secure happiness that surrounded the children playing there. It should be a good place to teach in.

Of course, the first thing I wanted to do was look at the flat above the stables. It had a sitting room, a double bedroom, a kitchen and a bathroom, that would make a perfect home for us, once the place was redecorated. Meanwhile, Strix was letting us have a bedroom in the main building, until the flat was ready. I met the rest of the staff at our meeting the next day, and heard the teaching timetable I would be following. It was basically general subjects, for a class of ten seven year olds, so it should not present any real problems. The staff were an interesting mixture of qualified and unqualified teachers, and I was somewhere in the middle. I had done a year in a Froebel school in Buckinghamshire, plus the governess experience in the United States, and I really enjoyed teaching. I was to be paid a small amount, but Paul's schooling and the flat were free, and Ernest's salary from his civil service job in Scotland Yard, would give us a reasonably good income.

Edna was in charge of the academic side of the school, and she was the ex-wife of the African leader, Jomo Kenyatta. She had a son of Paul's age, called Peter, who was already very good at sport, and as bright as a button in lessons. He was Paul's special friend, and, on sports' day, they took the honours between them. Edna had very fond memories of Jomo, whom she had met when she was training to be a teacher.

He had courted her enthusiastically, but she thought they would not have married if her parents had not both been killed by a random buzz bomb. She had felt alone, and very sad, and was persuaded to make, what had seemed to be, a passing relationship, permanent. Since Jomo was alive, and very active in Kenyan politics, I asked her if she would go back to him, if the opportunity arose. She gave a definite, "Yes!" to the question, adding that if he just lifted his little finger, she would be at his side immediately.

Sarah was very keen on teaching English, and especially enjoyed work in speech training. She was tall and well-built, and the daughter of one of the surgeons at Guy's Hospital. Her uncle was a famous QC, and her sister, Mary, had married a television personality, whom she had met in very romantic circumstances. She was going up one escalator at King's Cross, and the TV game presenter was going down the other one. Their eyes met across the central banister, and they fell in love. Mary waited at the top, and when he reached the bottom of his staircase, he came straight back up to speak to her. When Sarah told me the story I could scarcely believe it, but it was so improbable that she just couldn't have made it up, and when I finally met Mary, she confirmed that truth was, indeed, stranger than fiction.

Tessa was eighteen, and a teaching assistant, rather in the way I had been at Woodlands. After taking school certificate, she had left the local convent school, and, as her parents knew Strix, they had asked if their daughter could spend some time as an assistant at Pinewood, while she decided what she wanted to do as a career. She was a natural 'mother', although she was so young, and all the children adored her. She gave them the love that they were missing by being at boarding school, and Paul was one of her favourites. Tessa had a wonderful figure, with a tiny waist, which I greatly envied, as I was still a lot fatter than I had been when I went away. She also had an extremely good dress sense and always looked very smart, which wasn't easy when you're spending the day with adoring four year olds. Tessa already had several beaux, and I was pretty sure that her life's work would, in reality, turn out to be marriage and motherhood!

Once the decorating was done, we managed to furnish the flat from various auction sales, plus things we cadged from Buddy, and finished up with a very comfortable little home. Paul sometimes came to spend time with us in the evening, but we were pleased that he had friends among the other children, and often played with them until bedtime. He had a special 'girl friend' called Angela Pleasance, whose father was an actor, and who went on the stage herself, when she left school. Angela was very pretty, with lovely fair hair and bright blue eyes. Paul absolutely adored her.

All we now needed, to complete the picture of a happy family, was a dog, and for some reason that I can't remember, I decided that we should buy an English bull terrier. I think I had heard that they were intelligent and very good with children, so I found a breeder not too far away with puppies for sale. We had always had a male dog, but this time I chose a delightful little brindle bitch, who was half-sister to the champion of England. Her Kennel Club name was 'Araminta of Old Copper', and we bought her on, what were called, 'breeding terms'. That allowed the breeder to get her mated, and to have first pick of the resulting litter. We called her 'Minty', and she lived up to all our expectations. She was wonderful with the children, who all grew very fond of her, and she quickly learnt never to jump up on the little ones. She was as bright as Perry had been, but this time I didn't teach her tricks. I taught her obedience, which was considerably more useful.

Our social life also revolved around Pinewood. We met Tessa's parents and immediately liked them. They were a railway family and Freddie, her father, had been in charge of important admin in the LNER. Now that he had retired, he spent a lot of time organising sports events for teenagers. His father was a railwayman too, and, at nearly ninety, was chairman of the local education committee. Her mother's name was Doris, but I christened her 'Dimpy' as she had lovely dimples, and she was a superb cook. Dimpy made the most delicious blackcurrant pie I had ever tasted, and when we went to tea, she discovered that I loved cucumber sandwiches, so, whenever we called, a good supply was always ready.

Dimpy's friends, the Marques, owned the local firm, Concrete Utilities, which supplied local councils with the high concrete lamppost, for street lighting. They owned a beautiful house at Great Amwell, and we often played bridge there. Charlie Marques was a charming, dynamic Australian, who had lost the sight of one eye when he was chopping wood for some old people, and a splinter had flown up and pierced the eyeball. He still drove down the narrow Hertfordshire lanes like a bat out of hell, and I was amazed that he had never had an accident. They had two boys, and the elder son, Robin, was at university, planning on coming back later to manage the firm.

Great Amwell hosted a magical event every Midsummer Day. A choir of boys from Haileybury, the famous public school nearby, came to sing madrigals on a little island in the New River, which ran past the village. It was always a romantic evening, light till after ten, the reflections in the stream of the lanterns the boys carried, sparkling like floating diamonds. There was something unforgettable about the close harmony of the madrigals combined with the sweet scent of the many wild flowers that grew on the banks of the little river, under a starry night sky. After the concert, we would all go to the local pub for a drink to celebrate the occasion.

I'm sure that East Hertfordshire is still a very good place to live, but in 1948, it was mainly leafy countryside around pleasant little towns like Ware, Hertford and Sawbridgeworth. The pressure on planners to allow the building of houses, had not really begun, and pretty villages were, as yet, unspoiled by the addition of new estates, and all the supporting infrastructure. The Great Cambridge Road was only a single carriageway, and the M1 motorway, still just a dream in some transport engineer's eye.

In October, the green in the woods around the school began to turn to shades of orange with the onset of autumn, and Ernest told me that he dreaded the start of foggy winter evenings, with the inevitable train cancellations and delays. Buddy hated the winter, which made riding around on a bicycle, as district nurse, very hazardous on icy roads. However, November brought a welcome addition to the family, and a new first cousin for Paul. Peggy and Dick, over in Orpington, had a little boy on the 16th, they named 'Giles', just missing a shared birthday with Princess Elizabeth and Prince Philip's first baby, 'Charles', the future heir to the throne. It was a truly memorable year.

My next major project was to take the driving test, so that we could buy a cheap little car. I had my eye on an Austin Seven, and I was sure that the garage in Enfield would find one for me. It would, of course be pre-war, but there had been a huge number of non-essential cars laid-up during the war years, when petrol was strictly rationed, and many of these had barely been used. Every advertisement seemed to say, "Low mileage/ One lady owner!". I took a driving lesson before my test, just in case there were little things I ought to do, that probably had absolutely nothing to do with actually driving on the road. I had no doubt at all that I would pass easily, but I couldn't risk the fiasco of having to do the whole thing twice, just because of some silly omission on my part.

The test centre was on the other side of Enfield, so I chose a driving school near to it, in the hope that they would show me the actual test route. My instructor turned out to be a rather podgy middle-aged man, who looked as though he spent too much time eating, and not enough keeping fit. He was relieved when he discovered that I could actually drive, as he had been told it was a woman having her first lesson, which, clearly, would not have been his favourite kind of pupil. I liked the car, which was a Ford saloon, though it had, to my surprise, two steering wheels. One was for the driver, and there was another smaller one on the passenger side, so that the instructor could take control in an emergency.

I explained that I had been driving in New York City, but I needed a British licence before I bought a car, and wanted to know exactly how to pass the actual test. We did a tour around Bush Hill Park, and once he was satisfied that I really could drive, he gave me a series of useful tips, one of which concerned the rear view and wing mirrors. It seemed that you had to turn your head very obviously, so that you were seen to be constantly checking them, and I followed his advice so energetically that, by the time the lesson was over, my neck was killing me!

The second tip was how and when to use hand signals, as well as the indicators that flicked out from the sides of the car. I twice hit my hand on the glass as I prepared to wave it around outside the car, so I made a mental note to remember to open the window. To my slight relief, the parking manoeuvre from the New York test was not part of the British version, which only had a three-point turn in a road and a reverse around a corner. When we got back to the driving school, I promised to book the test as soon as possible, and told him I would like to take it in one of their cars It was no problem, so I thanked him and took the bus back to Enfield. Everything was going to plan.

The day of the test was foggy and when the driving school car pulled into the forecourt of the Test Centre, the examiner came out to meet us. He said that he thought conditions on the roads were too dangerous for the test, and he would arrange a new appointment. I was horrified, as that would mean asking Strix for another day off, and paying for a further use of the driving school car. I told the examiner that I very much wanted to go ahead, despite the fog, as I was not a learner driver and had had a full licence for over three months in the United States. After a brief pause, he agreed to try, on the understanding that if there were problems, we would instantly abandon the exam. I thanked him and we set off.

The fog got worse by the minute, but, in record time, we went around the test course. I gave constant glances into the car's mirrors, made hugely overstated hand signals, and after doing a quick three-point turn in a fairly narrow road, I knew that the ordeal was over. My examiner actually smiled, as he gave me the slip of paper that would be valid for the rest of my life, and then retreated quickly to his office, declaring that no further testing would take place, until the fog lifted. Ernest and Buddy were both very pleased when they heard the news as it meant that we could now have a car. Buddy even offered to lend me the money to buy one, so I quickly accepted.

The garage sold us a nice little Austin Seven, with a fabric body, and we were soon buzzing here, there and everywhere, without the need to hang about at bus stops. Petrol was not expensive, at about two shillings a gallon, or10p in today's currency, and though it was still rationed, there would be enough for us to use the car to go and see Buddy, or visit friends at weekends. I sometimes gave Sarah a lift home to Broxbourne, and one day she managed to tip the car into a ditch as she got out, so we bit the bullet and got something slightly bigger and a lot heavier. The new car was a 'Singer', like Buddy's sewing machine, and it went very well, so we kept it for the next six months.

Teaching at Pinewood was always interesting, but I knew that, at the end of the school year, I ought to go to college and get a qualification, if I was going to have a career in education. However, another project was taking shape in my mind, that perhaps this might be the moment to try the concept of a 'nappy service' in Enfield, run on the same lines as General Diaper Service, and making us into millionaires. I started, in secret, to plan how it could be done, and where I could get the money to do it.

We had a wonderful Christmas at Florence Avenue, and Buddy and Ernest seemed to get on really well together. Although he was only five, we took Paul to midnight mass and he managed to stay awake. We sang carols about peace on earth, which definitely sounded relevant, for the war was over, our problems solved, and the future in 1949 looked very hopeful. It seemed a good time to discuss, with Ernest, the idea of starting a nappy service. I wanted him to realise that it would have a lot going for it, as we could try to rent a shop, that had a flat above for us to live in. To my total surprise, he agreed.

Ernest had already worked out that, when the year at Pinewood ended, it would be necessary for us to find somewhere to live and that it would be helpful if I had a job. Paul would go to a nearby primary school, and become the very first of all the various cousins, to sample the state education system. Buddy liked the plan, when we told her what we were considering doing, partly because it would bring us closer if we came to Enfield, and partly because she, too, loved the thought of possible fame and fortune. Her father, a pharmacist, with a chemist's shop in Kingston on Thames, had definitely been an entrepreneur, and Buddy had been brought up to look for faults in things she bought, and to ask for a price reduction if she found one. His adage "Those who ask won't get, and those who don't ask don't want," had puzzled her when she was a little girl, and I could never make understand it either. He had died, a rich man, in 1937, so perhaps twelve years later, the Norris family might have a profitable future in business after all!

Chapter 20

The Spring Term at Pinewood was very enjoyable. We had a car, so we could go on jaunts to Hertford. to call on friends, and to Enfield for weekend visits to see Buddy. She was thoroughly enjoying life as a district nurse, and, as she covered the west side of the town, her area included outlying houses around 'The Robin Hood' pub, on the extreme outskirts of Enfield, and near Whitewebbs, a big country park. She had swapped her bicycle for a motorised 'autobike', as she would often have to travel several miles to get to a patient, but she soon began to have dreams of buying a little car, once she had passed the driving test.

On the face of it, the test should not have provided too great a hurdle. Buddy had a very good road sense, and was a confident rider of her autobike in quite heavy traffic. She knew the area well and was aware of awkward stretches of road that might be, potentially, dangerous. When she asked if I would give her lessons in our car, I was delighted to say yes. She had been tremendously helpful all the time I had been away, and I was glad to have a chance to say thank-you. It looked a fairly straightforward project, but it turned out to be 'Mission Impossible'.

We chose Sunday as the best time, as not many patients needed a visit from the district nurse. It was also the easiest day for me to have several hours free, and there was less traffic on the road. Our first lesson was a great success, as Buddy soon got the hang of exactly how to get the car into gear, and let the clutch out very slowly. We made a little trip along Florence Avenue in first gear, and all seemed set for a successful outcome. To cut a long story short, Buddy did manage to drive the car reasonably well and I passed on all my 'tips for the test' before the actual examination. We drove to the test centre, full of hope that we would be able to carry out the ceremonial tearing up of 'L plates', and start the search for Buddy to have nice little car of her own.

I waited for the triumphant return, but as soon as I saw the expression on her face, I had guessed that the news was not good. She came over with a piece of paper that gave the reason for her failure. It said she had mounted the curb when reversing round a corner, so we knew exactly which skill to concentrate on before the next driving test. I consoled her with the fact that more than fifty percent of learners failed their first test, and we would soon put matters right.

For the next three lessons we reversed around nearly every corner we came to, until she did it perfectly each time, and we went for her second test secure in the knowledge that, this time, she would succeed. Once again, her glum face told me the bad news and I wondered what had happened. She had failed the emergency stop. The examiner had rapped on the ledge in front of him, and she had briefly panicked. The pause in her response, meant that they travelled several yards before coming to a halt. Reversing had gone well, the three point turn had presented no problems, all her skills in traffic were good, but, alas, this one fault had deprived her of success.

Nothing daunted, we practised the emergency stop, until she did it so well that we could halt in less than the length of the car, and several times I was lucky not to hit my head on the windscreen. Now we were really all set for the much sought-after success that the third test would bring. Lots of cheerful 'third time lucky' good wishes, sent her off in the car with the examiner, and I waited to give her a congratulatory hug, but it was not to be. The despair was palpable when they returned. Even the examiner looked disappointed. It appeared that, in her anxiety to get everything exactly right, she had not noticed a red traffic light, and had driven straight through it. As an experienced road-user, she was furious with herself, and totally abandoned any idea of getting a car, so that was the end of the saga. The whole debacle was never mentioned again.

In late spring, there is nothing in the whole world to beat the beauty of the English countryside, and the woods around Great Amwell were full of bluebells. It was a very happy time for Ernest and for me, as all our disagreements had disappeared into a forgotten past, and there were exciting plans to be made for our future. The idea of a 'nappy service' had progressed to the point where I had worked out roughly how much it would cost, and how to raise the necessary funds.

We would rent the shop, with a flat above, and we could buy the necessary machines for 'the dirty work'! I remembered my 'laboratory tested' spiel for General Diaper Service, which promised no cross-infection between babies, and I was sure that we would need a steam sterilizer, to be absolutely certain that everything was medically kosher. Enquiries soon showed that such equipment was not cheap, and, with the washing and drying machines, the outlay would be quite considerable.

A delivery van was an absolute necessity, and mothers would want special waterproof containers for soiled nappy disposal, with removable bags ready for collection. There must be leaflets, detailing the advantages and cost of the service, and a shop front that attracted passing customers. I had learnt a lot about sales' promotion in New York, and I knew how vital a good, catchy name would be. One morning I woke up with a brilliant idea: "ROCKABYE NAPPY SERVICE" and the sales' message would be, "MAKE YOURS A ROCKABYE BABY!" All I needed now were funds to get things going when the school year ended, and a working partner to share the cash outlay.

In fact, I found an answer to both needs, close at hand. Tessa was teaching at Pinewood while she decided what to do for a career. She was young, jolly, and strong, and most important of all, we got on well together. I spoke to her about my ideas and she was tremendously enthusiastic. She thought that her grandfather might be interested in lending us her share of the money, while Buddy came up trumps, as usual, and offered the other half, so things were settled surprisingly quickly. I spent several Saturdays trawling the Enfield estate agents in an effort to find a suitable shop, but they were in short supply. The main problem was the living accommodation, as flats of all kinds were usually let on long term leases, and I got to know all about 'security of tenure' for sitting tenants.

Over the years, I had been very lucky in finding the right people, at the right moment, and this time I met Mr Holt. He was a partner, with a Mr Mabison, in an Enfield estate agency that managed quite a few commercial properties, and he thought he might be able to help. He was fascinated by the idea of a nappy service, and amused that anyone would be crazy enough to start one. There was a shop, he told me, in Baker Street, a fairly busy road just a few minutes from the centre of town, which had two flats above it. One, on the second floor, was let to protected tenants, a couple with a baby, and the rest of the premises was made up of a substantial shop with a large store room, and living accommodation over two floors. A sitting room and kitchen, were at the back on the ground floor, plus three bedrooms and a bathroom, on the first floor. Would Ernest and I like to see it? I could have hugged him!

Baker Street led, through Silver Street, into the town centre of Enfield, past residential roads with historic names like Monastery Gardens. We saw a mixture of houses and businesses until, around 'The Hop Poles', it was only made up of small shops. I noticed that there was a vacant lot, covered in grass and weeds, next to 'our' shop, so there would be off-street parking. Mr Holt let us in through the shop door and I could see, immediately, that it would suit us down to the ground. It was really spacious, and the store room was big enough to take all our machines, with a wash basin and lavatory attached, so neither water nor drainage access would be a problem.

The living room, with a door leading into a little kitchen, had a proper fireplace and a big sash window, overlooking a sizeable yard. We went upstairs to find that the three bedrooms were perfectly adequate, and the bathroom was surprisingly big, having probably once been a fourth bedroom. On the landing, a narrow, steep staircase led to a door, which we were told was the entry into the top flat. This meant that the tenants would have to come through the shop to reach it, but that was a minor problem. Mr Holt said that we could have a twelve month lease, to be re-negotiated after a year, and when he told us the rent, we knew that we just had to say yes, immediately. It would be a double success; a new home and a new enterprise, in one fell swoop!

Buddy was absolutely delighted when she heard the good news, as Baker Street was a mere five minute bike ride from Florence Avenue. Tessa and her grandfather were shown around by Mr Holt, and they could see how well the shop would work as a headquarters for 'Rockabye Nappy Service'. The spring term had just ended at Pinewood, so Tessa and I told Strix that we would both be leaving in July. She was very interested in our plans for the future though she had never heard of the idea of a nappy service, and wished us luck, with, I suspected, her fingers well and truly crossed.

The Easter holidays brought a flurry of activity, as we started to set up the new business. Tessa and I went up to the Marylebone Road, to the sellers of medical equipment, to buy the steam steriliser, and look at commercial washing and drying machines, and Ernest got interested in the printing of promotional leaflets. Buddy promised to notify all the local maternity units of the new service that would be available from September, and put up her share of the investment without hesitation. She was behind us in every way, getting Paul registered at 'Merryhills', the best local primary school, with a catchment area of desirable private houses on the way to Enfield West Underground station.

Buddy asked one favour, that I should take her to see the family grave at Rickmansworth, where my father, and my little sister, Betty, were both buried. I was really pleased to drive there from Enfield, as the car had opened all sorts of opportunities to do new things, and I had not seen the grave since I left school. Betty had died at five and a half, in the December, as I was born the following July, and we must have been conceived at about the same time of the year, as her birthday was on July 16th, two days after mine. I had always thought I would have really loved having her as a big sister, as she had golden hair and beautiful blue eyes.

We set off from Buddy's house after an early lunch, leaving Ernest in charge of Paul, and we got to Rickmansworth by three in the afternoon, which seemed very good going. We stopped at a nursery to buy some plants for the grave, as Buddy was afraid that it would be overgrown with weeds after such a long time. They had lots of trays of young asters, which had been one of my father's favourite flowers, and were fairly hardy. At the same time we saw trays of Brussels sprouts, also in the two leaf stage, so we bought some for the garden at Florence Avenue, as Buddy had started a little vegetable plot and sprouts were easy to grow.

Once we had got to the cemetery, we parked the car and started the search for the grave, which was not easy as there were masses of grassy mounds, and Buddy had not been able to afford a tombstone when my father died. When she did have enough money, she said she felt it was too late to disturb the earth, so the grave was unmarked. Fortunately the cemetery keeper was on hand, and he looked up the plot number in his records and showed us where it was. We had brought a trowel with us, so we set to, taking out the weeds and grasses and planted our little asters in neat parallel lines. Buddy did not like the modern 'natural' look, and each little plant had its own space, ready for the spreading flowers that would come in July and August.

We were both pleased with our gardening efforts and had an enjoyable journey home, during which she regaled me with stories of Betty, and what a sweet little girl she had been. Ernest and Paul had enjoyed their afternoon together, and Buddy accepted his offer to plant the sprouts in the new vegetable plot. Ernest liked neat rows too, and the plants looked very healthy, so we looked forward to some delicious meals with home grown Brussels from the garden. Alas, we never had them, for, instead, lines of brightly coloured asters appeared in Buddy's vegetable plot. I am sure there must be someone, somewhere, who still tells the unlikely story of the grave in Rickmansworth cemetery, where they once saw two neat lines of thriving Brussels sprouts, and though it seemed like sacrilege, even Buddy had to laugh.

My final term at Pinewood went by very quickly and there was a thoroughly enjoyable Sports' Day in the last week. Peter Kenyatta and Paul won all the five year old races, including the egg and spoon, and Tessa walked away with the staff trophy, which made her father and her grandfather, very proud. Ernest took a day off to umpire a cricket match between two parents' teams and I became a fortune teller for the day, raising money for the home for retired horses. It was great fun, wearing a Gypsy Rose Lee outfit, and sitting in a little tent with a crystal ball on a table in front of me. I read hands, and was surprised at how often people said, "Why, that's absolutely right!" when I mentioned hopes and dreams they might have. Probably that was because I only told them nice things, and carefully avoided the gypsy's warning.

We had arranged for a van to come and pick up our stuff, for the move to Enfield, so when all the redecoration of the living area was finished, we packed up all our bits and pieces and took possession of our first real family home in the Baker Street shop. Amazingly, we already seemed to have a lot of furniture, and decided not to buy too much more until we found how things turned out. There was a big sale room at the top of Silver Street, with auctions every Thursday, and when we needed something, I could always go and try to find a bargain buy. I still have two things I bought at sales there in 1948, a standing ashtray in the form of a black waiter, that we named 'Joseph', and an Indian brass table top, that makes a wonderful fire screen.

Once we had moved in and got the living accommodation sorted out, Tessa and I got to work on starting the business. I exchanged the car for a little van, and we found a sign writer to decorate the sides with a design of a baby lying joyfully in a hammock, slung between two blossoming branches. The words 'Rockabye Nappy Service' floated below, and the whole thing was very twee, but meant to attract young mothers.The van was a very good buy, and we kept it until I left Trent Park four years later, where the design on the side caused a great deal of amusement.

Just before we had actually moved, I met the top floor tenants, who were now our responsibility. Mr and Mrs Tully were not an attractive couple. She was slightly emaciated, with thin, faded fair hair, a pale face, and already, in her late twenties, had started to look careworn, whereas her husband appeared to be a spiteful bully, who obviously kept her well under his thumb. The baby boy was the image of his mother, and he looked pathetic, wrapped in a slightly grubby shawl. The man soon left us, saying that he was meeting someone at the pub, and warned her not to keep him waiting for his dinner, when he got back later.

Mrs Tully said that they were on the waiting list for a council house, but so were a lot of other people, though the fact that they had a baby would give them extra 'points'. She told me that she had to stay awake every night as she was afraid that her heart might stop, if she went to sleep. and she might die. She had to keep checking that it was still beating. I felt desperately sorry for her and her baby, and doubted whether she would get a lot of sympathy from her unpleasant husband, so I told her not to hesitate to come and talk to me, if it would help in any way. Needless to say, she never did, but we offered her a little cleaning job in the shop, and in our part of the house, which cheered her up considerably, as it meant she had a little money of her own. For the record, they were still waiting for that council house when we moved to Cheshunt, four years later.

Chapter 21

We had set September 1st, Buddy's birthday, for the start of the actual nappy service, so that just left August, to find some customers and get everything sorted out. There was a lot that Tessa and I knew nothing about, so we were on a steep learning curve, getting to understand things like liquid detergents, and the temperatures at which the steam sterilizer should be set. A lot of salesmen called to try to get our custom, and we were able to get good bargains in the metal containers for the soiled nappies, with waterproof lining bags for collection by the van. The detergent came in giant bottles that would have to be decanted into something that Tessa and I could manage, and Ernest did as much as he could at weekends, when he didn't have to go to London.

Most families did not have washing machines in 1948, but relied on 'laundrettes' for things they didn't wash at home. There were no such things as 'disposable nappies', so I was optimistic that we would be able to find enough customers to make the service profitable. The leaflets turned out very well, and we did a door to door drop in affluent houses, where there were babies. I followed that with a personal call two or three days later, and we had gathered about half a dozen orders to start in September.

At the beginning of August, I got a very strange letter, forwarded from Pinewood. It was from Dave, who had come from Washington to the goodbye gathering on the QE, and I was totally amazed at the contents. He had got my address from Bob and Mary, and reminded me that I had said that, if he ever came to England, he should look me up, and, by the time I got the letter, he would be halfway across the Atlantic, to make a surprise visit. Worse still, he wanted me to book a room for 'us' in London, so that we could spend time together. I should meet the train at Victoria, and we could go straight to the hotel.

In a way, I was hoist with my own petard! It had seemed totally unnecessary to explain to Dave my reason for being in the USA, and though Bob and Mary knew about Ernest, I had not mentioned him to anyone else. Everyone had heard all about Paul, as I kept his photograph in my wallet, but I had never, at any time, been other than cheerfully friendly with Dave. I immediately told Ernest all about him, but, in fact, there was nothing to tell, and he said I must meet the train, and tell Dave the whole story. I could see that he was quietly amused when he realised how much I was dreading getting my comeuppance

In fact, it was so totally embarrassing, that it was almost funny. I had booked a room for Dave in a guest house in the Paddington area, and duly went to Victoria, to welcome him to England. I was very keen to avoid the intimacy of the back of a cab, and I needed time to tell him about Ernest, so, after a quick greeting, I suggested that we go by bus, so that he could get his first impression of London, from the top of a double-decker. He was looking very excited, and thoroughly enjoying our 're-union', and he readily agreed.

It was a journey I shall never forget. We got two seats on the top deck, right at the front, and as the bus pulled out of Victoria Station, I immediately started my explanation. Dave had a very strong southern accent, and quite a loud American voice, so very soon, everyone on the top of that bus was listening to our conversation. I had started by reminding him that I had a son, but he thought that I was about to confess that Paul was illegitimate. It didn't matter one little bit, he said, he understood how such things could have happened during the war.

At this point, the conductor arrived to collect our fare, so there was a pause in my story. However, I pressed on and explained that, in fact, I actually had a very nice husband, Paul's father, who was really looking forward to meeting my visiting American friend. Dave let out a cry of horror that would have stopped the bus if the driver had heard it "Oh, God! You've got a husband? Oh, my God!" There was total silence on the top of the bus. Even the conductor was no longer clipping tickets, and people were staring in our direction, waiting for the drama to unfold. The bus stopped, but no-one got off. This was, obviously, too good to miss!

Actually, the main feature was over, and the rest was just a B movie. Though reassured that Ernest really would love to meet him, and I would introduce them at the weekend, Dave still seemed unconvinced. He said he was upset because his friends had all thought that he was going 'to bring that little English girl back to America', and now what would they say? I made him laugh by suggesting that they might tell him he had had a very lucky escape, and as we left the bus, quite a lot of the passengers were smiling. I almost expected a little burst of applause!

Leaving him at the hotel, I hurried back to Enfield to tell Ernest the outcome of my adventure. He offered a good idea. Since we were not getting a summer holiday, we could rent a flat by the sea for a long weekend, and take Dave with us. Perhaps he might meet a different little English girl to console him. Brighton would be a good place, though, as it was August, we could probably only hope to find a cancellation.

The following day I had arranged to meet Dave to go to the London Zoo, as the first of several places I thought he might enjoy. I loved the zoo, but for the first time ever, the visit ended in just over an hour. I guided him first into the lion house, which I had always thought was a really exciting experience. He gave the lions a cursory glance, and then made the memorable comment, "Yes, I've seen a lion before!" The tigers and the polar bears were similarly dismissed, and it took a huge bird-eating spider in the Insect House, to get any real reaction. Even feeding time at the seal enclosure, became a non-event, so we went to have our own lunch in the zoo restaurant, where I told him about the idea for a short stay on the coast.

Ernest had managed to find a two bedroom apartment in Brighton that we could rent for the following weekend, if Dave was interested in a breath of English sea air. I suggested that he should come to Enfield to meet Ernest, say a quick 'hullo' to Paul, and then the three of us could go on to Sussex in comfort, in a hired car. It was an attractive thought from my point of view, as we had accepted that we would be too busy to have a holiday before 'Rockabye' got underway, and this would give us a little calm before the storm. Dave quite liked the general idea of going to a seaside resort, though he was still doubtful about Ernest's possible reaction to him. I assured him that the three of us would get on splendidly, and, maybe, we could even lay on a brief romantic interlude for him in Brighton.

Taking Paul with me, I met his train in Enfield on the Thursday afternoon, and they were soon great friends, as Dave had brought him a swish cowboy outfit from America. Ernest arrived home for supper and got on very well with Dave, as they swapped stories of the lack of appreciation of the sterling work Civil Servants did, on both sides of the Atlantic. We had dropped Paul off at Florence Avenue, the previous evening, and Dave had met Buddy, who thanked him for his kindness to me in Washington. I was relieved to see, he was really pleased with his reception by my entire family. On the journey, Dave told Ernest about the agonies of being an alcoholic, the awful desire to go on drinking without any joy or release from the problems of living, I just hoped we could find someone in Brighton to give him a good time.

The flat was fine, and just off the sea front, so we decided to change and go to a thé dansant nearby, where there should be ready-made partners to keep Dave happy. Indeed there were, because for every man there seemed to be at least two girls. Ernest was not an enthusiastic dancer, but we waltzed around cheerfully, and to our relief Dave had soon picked up two or three girls. One attractive blonde seemed to have taken his fancy, and he introduced us as they came off the dance floor. She was a local girl called Maureen, who had had several glasses of sherry, and was holding his arm quite firmly. Ernest and I decided that this was the moment for us to make a speedy exit, and let him get on with the business in hand, whatever that was. We said goodbye, with an optimistic whisper of, "See you tomorrow!", and went back to the flat.

We had a pleasant stroll along the promenade, and were wondering whether to go and see a film or just have an early night, when the front door opened and Dave appeared. He had taken Maureen home in a taxi when the dance ended, and it turned out that she lived with her mother, over a dairy. His hopes were high as she was getting quite affectionate, so he was expecting an invitation to go in with her and have a coffee. Poor old Dave's luck was out! Maureen gave him a quick kiss, and said she was sorry but she couldn't ask him in, because her mother wouldn't like it, and immediately shut the door. Ten days later, at the end of his visit to England, we went up to have dinner with him in London. He said he had had a wonderful holiday that he would never forget and promised to keep in touch. I certainly thought we would see him again, but, as before, I was quite wrong!

The start of the delivery and collection of nappies began, as promised, on Wednesday, September 1st. As always, I bought Buddy a bouquet of large bronze chrysanthemums, and we all sang 'Happy Birthday' to mark the occasion. She was admitting to being 59, though a glance at her birth certificate would have added an extra five years. I had delivered the metal cans and bags for the soiled nappies a week earlier, and from now, on there would be a twice a week collection and delivery service. As we were supplying both towelling and Harrington squares, we proudly took the first parcel of shining white nappies to six welcoming front doors. We were very hopeful that, once the satisfied customers spread the word, we would be overwhelmed with orders.

Tessa was a very good business partner, in that she was young, and therefore malleable, and like me, she was totally committed to the success of the venture. We shared the dreary washing, sterilizing and drying chores, though, because I was out on the round, she was in charge of the day to day schedule in the shop. We had expected problems with the careless rinsing of 'dirty' nappies, but that rarely happened, and we soon got into a routine that worked. The industrial washing and drying machines did a good job, and the steam sterilizer appeared more complicated than it actually was.

We ironed the Harrington squares, to make them look better, and with the carefully folded the terry towel nappies, they were wrapped in brown paper, ready for delivery. After about a month, I knew why the milkman's horse moved to the next house on the round, without prompting. I had my route, and it remained unchanged, apart from the addition of a new customer. One Sunday, when I was driving alone to go somewhere totally unconnected with the Nappy Service, I let my thoughts wander, and before I realised it, I had pulled up outside the first house on my 'Rockabye' round.

We all worked hard, including little Paul, who sometimes, as van boy, would knock on the customer's front door to deliver the fresh supply. He had a prepared greeting that began, "Good morning, madam, ..." After one call, he came back to the van, very worried, as a man had answered the door. Paul hoped he had done the right thing, "I said 'good morning, madam', but it was a sir!"

Tessa had a new suitor, a very personable, young vet, whom she had met in Hertford. She was very keen on horses, and several of her friends had their own ponies, all of which needed veterinary care at one time or the other. Andy was from Northern Ireland, with all the charm and energy that the Irish often display, and I liked him immediately. Our bull terrier, Minty, suddenly received VIP treatment, that required constant visits. Inoculations, nail trimming, inspections of teeth, you name it, Minty got it all, either free for a friend, or at the cost of the medication. Naturally, the presence of the vet was mandatory, and I was an interested observer of some extremely committed courting.

A few weeks after the start of 'Rockabye', Paul caught mumps at school, and shortly afterwards passed the infection on to Ernest. Buddy swung into action, helping to nurse the two invalids, but fortunately both Tessa and I had had the disease as children, the business was not affected. Poor old Ernest suffered the misery that is the adult male's experience of inflamed glands, and he took much longer than Paul to recover. However, he did everything he could to help, ironing nappies, doing the shopping, and looking after Paul, and it was great to have his company during the day.

Time was passing but, despite all our efforts, the nappy service was still not breaking even. The cost of rent, detergent, electricity and petrol, was more than the money coming in from customers. Neither Tessa nor I was taking any salary or expenses, and luckily our backers were my mother and her grandfather, or we would have soon gone bankrupt. We needed more customers, but how we could get them, was not immediately apparent. We had leafleted the whole district, and Buddy had made sure that all the local midwives knew about the wonderful service 'Rockabye' gave. We had set the price at a reasonable level, and, as we were already losing money, it did not make sense to make it cheaper.

The awful truth had started to dawn on me, that not enough mothers in Enfield wanted to invest in nappy service. It could be that in Chelsea, or Kensington, where salaries were higher, it would have worked. All I knew was that, after five months of doing everything possible to succeed, we had failed. It was a very bitter pill to swallow. Everyone had done their absolute best. Tessa had, uncomplainingly, shouldered the main burden of nappy washing; Ernest had helped in every way he could, and he was the sole wage earner in the family, while Buddy did her best to support us, by cheerfully calling in at the shop, and encouraging us to keep the flag flying. I knew that it was my idea, and so there was no way to pass the buck. It would be my fault if our two backers lost most of the cash that they had, so trustingly, invested.

Looking back over the years, I realise that 'Rockabye' was probably doomed from the start. Nappy washing had always been seen, in the middle class families we were trying to sell to, as one of a mother's duties, and to trust it to any outside agency could have seemed irresponsible. Cross-infection might be an ever present risk, despite assurances on steam sterilizing techniques. In the United States, diaper service had been going for years and people were used to the concept, but in England it was just another new-fangled idea, costing money that could be better used for something else.

It certainly did not help that 1948 was the beginning of the popularity and affordability of automatic washing machines,. and they were available on hire-purchase. The machines could do all the family's laundry, including nappies, while washing powders were attractively advertised, promising 'a whiter than white' wash, as a do-it-yourself incentive. Tessa and I talked interminably about rescue plans, but, in the end, there was only one possible course of action. 'Rockabye Nappy Service' would have to cease trading.

Once we had come to the decision, we agreed that we would slowly wind-down the business, and warn our existing customers of our intentions. They all took it very well, assuring us that they had tremendously appreciated the service we had given, and hoping that a miracle would come to save us. They recognised how hard we had tried to succeed, and realised that our hopes were now a thing of the past. We had to deal with a rather bleak financial future. Buddy, as usual, turned up trumps, and we insisted that Tessa's grandfather should get back the capital he had invested, and she would bear the loss. After all, it had been my idea.

A frequent visitor at that time, whose company I really enjoyed, was Peggy's husband, Dick. I had always liked him and when he came for a weekend stay, Ernest and I would play cards with him, and laugh a lot, which helped us to forget the gathering clouds of financial meltdown. He would come from Orpington by car, which was quite a long drive, but he was cheerful and positive and we loved his visits. He had settled down wonderfully well after the traumas of the war, and had restarted his career as an architect with a firm in London, so all seemed set for a happy future.

One of the main business expenses in Enfield had been the rent of the shop, so we came to the decision that we could try to sub-let it, and here my contact with Mr Holt was invaluable. We desperately needed to keep the living accommodation, so he found us a tenant who sold and repaired radios, and who was willing to wait for a month to give us time to clear away all the nappy service machines. We ran a three day sale when we sold off nappies, containers, bottles of detergent, and anything moveable, like chairs and tables. For the very first time we had actual queues of customers, an accolade the nappy service had never managed to achieve! The washing and drying machines we sold second hand, and in the case of the steam sterilizer, the firm that had sold it to us, bought it back.

We kept the van, which was an invaluable substitute for a car, but everything else went towards repaying Tessa's grandfather, what we felt was, a debt of honour In the end, he only lost just over two hundred pounds, and was quite unhappy that he had not been asked to share the financial disaster. He felt that it had been a really worthwhile attempt at starting a business from scratch, and that Tessa had benefited from the experience. I certainly had, and, for the first time, realised the difficulties of working for yourself, with no assured income at the end of the week, however hard you tried. I never did it again!

Tessa had been a Trojan. She was always cheerful when things went wrong, as they frequently did. Once, when the machine wouldn't work, we held nappies in front of the electric fire to dry them. It took hours, but we could both see the funny side of the ridiculous situation, and ended up laughing so much that the tears ran down our cheeks. Even better, her romance with Andy, the vet, had progressed to thoughts of marriage, so I was very sure she would have a happy and settled future.

Ernest was a tower of strength, and very philosophical about what had happened to all my high hopes. He knew that Rockabye had not failed for lack of effort, so he just waited for my next career move, and hoped it would be more successful. In a way, he had quite enjoyed the excitement of starting a business, and had certainly played a big part in getting things going. We had a home, albeit at the back of a shop, but it was our home, and we had enjoyed living there as a little family. Of course, he still had the odd spat with Buddy, but their disagreements quickly evaporated in a way that they had not done when we lived under the same roof.

On the whole, things had turned out reasonably well, and I had made one major decision. I had tried lots of jobs, and in a way I had enjoyed them all. Nursing had been rewarding, but the thought of spending three more years as a probationer, was not an attractive proposition. Office work had only ever been fun in the company of amusing men, and though I had found sales' promotion an interesting challenge it was not an attractive way of spending the rest of my working life, while my recent failure as an entrepreneur had left an indelible mark. The one thing I really thought I might be able to do well, was teach. School had always been a happy place for me, whether it was the Convent, or Woodlands or Pinewood, but I needed to take a proper training, whatever that involved, and join the profession that had always fascinated my father.

By chance, within easy travelling distance of Enfield, there was a comparatively new teacher training college, that had been set up, specifically, to boost the number of teachers needed for the post-war expansion of the education system. It was called 'Trent Park Training College', after the lovely house in acres of beautiful parkland, that formed the central core of the campus, and I discovered that there was a secondary school course in 'English with Drama'. What more could I want? I put in an application and it was accepted.

My future was settled, and it was a decision I never regretted, for, in retrospect, I realise that I went into teaching with some basic skills that proved to be invaluable. I was used to living and working as part of a team, and understood the hierarchy that exists in all professions. I had really enjoyed my own school days and was sure that education should certainly be a mixture of business and pleasure.

The keeping of ledgers, all those years before, made the school register seem important, and I took a pride in its neatness and accuracy, that I soon discovered was not shared by some of my teaching colleagues!. As a nurse, I had known what it was to get physically tired, but stay cheerful. A hard day in school was rarely a problem, and I never lost the impatience I felt with staff who gave up the minute things got a bit tough, and took several days off to recover. Quite surprisingly, my most useful contribution to school turned out to be that I knew how to sell. Sales' promotion had taught me how to get things done by persuasion, and I thoroughly enjoyed the challenge of overcoming pupils' sales' resistance to being educated.

I certainly loved being a teacher, and even after thirty years on the journey from assistant to senior mistress, I still quite often said, "And to think they actually pay me!".

Chapter 22

"I wonder what happened to him?", one of Noel Coward's very witty songs for a West End review, began:

"Whatever became of old Archie? I hear he departed this life, After rounding-up ten sacred cows in Karachi, To welcome the Governor's wife!

IN AMERICA.........

Whatever became of BOB & MARY EFRON?

Very exciting things certainly happened to Bob and Mary. As soon as they both qualified, they married, and in 1953, they had a baby they named Carol. To my delight, Bob got a research fellowship to come to England, and work at the National Hospital for Nervous Diseases, in Queen's Square. His chosen specialisation was neurology, and he clearly had a high profile career in front of him. They had rented a large house in Finchley, and they both travelled every day to Queen's Square, with Mary giving her services free to a nearby hospital, and undertaking a study of urinary amino acid disorders.

We saw a great deal of them, both in Finchley and in Cheshunt, where we lived, and our close friendship has lasted right through to the end of all our lives. Ernest was absolutely fascinated by this pair of brilliant, amusing Americans, and we both realised that, if I hadn't gone to the States, we wouldn't have got to know them. They were very competitive with each other and I have never enjoyed games of Scrabble so much, as I did when we played with them. Perhaps in the fun of beating each other, there was already the shadow of disagreements that would ultimately cause them to part. For the moment life was wonderful, and the arrival of their second baby in 1955, was a truly happy event. Mary phoned to ask if they could call the little boy 'Paul', after our Paul, in the hope that he would turn out to be equally charming, and we were delighted to agree!

Bob's main investigation was in the brain, particularly in the function of memory, and he told us stories of experiments using cats and monkeys that made my blood run cold. Quite often the National Hospital would have an open discussion of various neurological problems, using a volunteer patient. These sessions were intended for medical students, but because I had a nursing background, Bob managed to get permission to take me to one. It was tremendously interesting, and the patient, a woman in her forties, was told to stretch an arm right out to the side, and then bring an extended fore- finger back to touch her nose. Each time, her finger missed her nose by some way, which obviously meant something, but she was smiling and cooperative and clearly enjoyed the limelight. When I got home we all tried it, and had absolutely no problems, so we were relieved to know that, at least, we hadn't got whatever she had !

One of Bob's experiments concerned a brain activity known as an 'alpha rhythm', and he asked everyone to volunteer to be tested. It only involved watching a screen on which images appeared in different depths, and the idea was to say which was the farthest away and which the nearest. Of course Ernest and I took part, and the results were very interesting. I went first, and couldn't see what problem anyone could have identifying which was which, but when it was Ernest's turn, he was completely unable to see any difference in depth between the images. It seemed he did not have an alpha rhythm. Bob reassured him that the lack of one did not matter at all, but it explained why, when Ernest went to watch a 3D film, using special viewing glasses, he could not understand why other people kept ducking to avoid the arrows, that the Red Indians seemed to be shooting at them.

It was in the course of investigating vision that Bob thought he had discovered how movies could be specially shot, to give a full 3D effect. For a moment, it looked as though he had struck scientific gold. At the time, 1955, Mike Todd, the flamboyant director, and husband of Liz Taylor, was planning to film the spectacular 'Round the World in 80 Days', and as soon as he got wind of Bob's research, he immediately arranged to meet him to discuss the commercial possibilities. If it really worked, the idea would be worth millions. Todd was already exploring innovative filming techniques in Cinerama, with the American Optical company, and a method called Todd/AO was finally used in the film.

Unfortunately, after several accidents including equipment catching fire and the explosion of the quartz additions to camera lenses, the search for a 3D process had to be abandoned. However, Bob had, by that time, been invited to one of Mike Todd's legendary parties and had danced with Liz Taylor, not to mention the excitement of the possibilities of riches galore, so he always remembered the contacts he made, with great affection. Mike Todd's death in a plane crash in 1958, shattered any remaining hopes, and Bob resumed his career as a neurologist, in which he was to become a world authority in several specialised areas.

MARY was every bit as successful in the long term, for her work in amino acids led to vast improvements in the care and prevention of many inherited diseases, particularly in the paediatric field in which she specialised. She saved innumerable lives, but by a terrible irony, she died by the actions of her own immune system. She was only thirty-nine when she developed lupus, a condition in which the body destroys itself, rejecting its own organs as if they were invaders. She had told me earlier, that she was splitting up with Bob, which had made me very sad, but I let her know that I would not be taking sides in their disagreement, and planned to stay close to both of them.

They had had a second daughter, they named Lucy, in 1959, and, after the divorce, Mary was given custody of the three children. Bob did everything he could to support them financially, but when she married again, it was all too clear that things were not right, and the children begged to be allowed to live with their father. Tragically, she died in 1967, though in her last days I was able to keep her plied with cheerful letters about things that happened at school, or to our family. Even though I knew that she would not recover, it was still a devastating blow when her new husband phoned to tell me she had died. I was very, very fond of her.

Her work at Queen's Square was just the beginning of research that led to worldwide recognition of the vital part that amino acids played in various congenital diseases. Scientific papers have recorded the debt medical knowledge owed to her, and in 2006, Bob and the children went to a ceremony in which she was posthumously awarded a well-deserved place in West Virginia's Hall of Fame.

Mary had an ingenuous enthusiasm that made all contacts with her great fun, and often surprising. Bob told the story of the time when they were with the three children, on a beach in Italy, and some youths, playing football nearby, were causing continuous annoyance. The ball was being kicked quite hard and kept landing dangerously near where the family were sitting. Though asked to be more careful, the group continued to threaten the children and Mary lost patience. The next time the ball landed near, she picked it up and ran away with it, hotly pursued by angry Italian teenagers. Bob was furious, as he could not leave the children alone, and was forced to watch, worrying what would happen when the chase ended. In fact, Mary was very fit and outdistanced her pursuers, throwing the ball away en route.   We were all very amused when, on a visit to Cheshunt, she told Buddy that Paul, then only three, was very constipated. Buddy suggested that the use of a piece of soap might be the answer. This puzzled Mary,. "I can't get him to eat his cornflakes," she queried, "How on earth shall I get him to eat soap?!" When we told her what had to be done with the soap, she laughed just as much as we did!

Whatever became of E.C. MULLENDORE?

It was in 1947, in Arkansas, that I had met E C.Mulendore. The McNulty family were very closely related, as his father, Gene, and Patience McNulty, were brother and sister, so we travelled the sixty or so miles to visit them at Thanksgiving. The Mullendores owned the largest ranch in Arkansas and E C, though only nine, drove his sister to school every day. The ease with which he drove the car impressed me at the time, and was a main factor in my success in the driving test in New York. ("If a boy of nine can do it, I certainly can!") Apart from that, I virtually forgot his existence, until one day in 2009, in mid Atlantic, when we were having lunch on Cunard's Queen Mary 2. Some other guests at the table said that they were from Oklahoma, and we started talking about the area around Tulsa, which I knew from my stay there, years before.

By an amazing coincidence they wanted to know if I had ever met the Mullendore family ? When I said I had, they asked if I knew that E C. had been shot, 'killed by persons unknown' in September, 1970. They told us that a book had been written about the circumstances of his death, entitled 'The Mullendore Murder Case', and, as soon as we got back home, Paul managed to buy a copy on line, and it had a very unhappy ending.

As his father, Gene, grew older, E.C. took over the running of the ranch and it proved necessary to borrow millions of dollars to pay day to day expenses. To secure these loans, huge insurance cover was taken out on E.C's life, to a final total of ten million dollars. He had other problems, in that he was drinking heavily and his wife, Linda, was suing for divorce. After a catalogue of disasters, E.C. was killed on the ranch by a mystery intruder, who shot him at point blank range. Several suspects were considered in the ensuing police investigation, but no-one was ever charged, and the crime remains unsolved. There was even the possibility that the Mafia might have been involved, for E.C.'s murder was certainly related to the huge amounts of money he had borrowed.

In the end, perhaps the greatest coincidence of all, was that I ever heard the story. The QM2 has over two thousand five hundred passengers, and meal-times are spread out over two hours in several venues. The seating at lunch is random, so that the chance of meeting any particular passenger is very, very small. The odds of being seated at the same table, at the same time, must be at least several thousands to one, yet it happened, so that we know what actually happened to E.C.

Whatever became of THE McNULTY FAMILY?

In 1998, Paul and I paid a visit to Cleveland, the small town in Oklahoma where I once lived with the McNulty's. The house was easy to find, but we wanted to discover what had happened to the family, so we went to the offices of the Town Council. No-one there had even heard of them, but someone suggested that the local estate agency might be able to help. It was a good idea, as the manager was in his early seventies, and had known the family well, especially Patience, whose parents had built the house before the.war, after they struck oil.

It seemed that, in the 1970s, McNulty had been killed in a riding accident, and the family had left Oklahoma. When asked what had happened, he told us that McNulty had been wearing spurs, and the horse had thrown him, and bolted. When he failed to return home, an alarm was raised and a search party found his body, lying in a field. We got the impression that the agent's sympathies were with the horse, which was unharmed.

Apparently, Patience decided to take the two children back to their home in New York City, and nothing more had been heard from them. When, at the end of our holiday in the States, we returned to New York, we tried, without success, to locate the McNulty's, but ran out of time, and so, finally, it had to be the end of the story!

A SALUTE TO TOSHIBA

I'm amazed to be reporting that I've had a change of mind,
For the angry words in 'Serenade' are now all sweet and kind!
It's very clear the hate I felt for laptops wasn't right
And so I want you all to know my genuine delight
That Tosh and I, in partnership, however strange it looks,
Have told the story of my life in two revealing books!

The first was 'Just Inside My Head', that spoke of happy times,
In Cheshunt, and the fun we had (plus entertaining rhymes!)
But, then, this tale of long ago gave you a second choice,
To read about my earlier days, in this, 'I See a Voice!'
And now that you've read Volume Two and made it to the end,
The dedication is

'For Paul'

(and you as well, dear friend!)

Folkestone, 2011